SUSTAINABLE BUSINESS STRATEGIES.

"Navigating the Green Horizon: A Guide to Building Resilient and Profitable Businesses through Sustainable Practices"

BY

ABAWULOR MOSES OMENKA .

COPYRIGHT.

Thank you for your understanding and compliance with copyright law, ensuring the continued protection of creative works and fostering a culture of respect for intellectual property.

CHAPTER ONE.

INTRODUCTION.

In a world where businesses face ever-growing challenges and opportunities, the pursuit of sustainable practices has emerged as a cornerstone for long-term success. This ebook, "Sustainable Business Practices for Long-Term Success," delves into the dynamic intersection of responsible business strategies and enduring profitability.

At the core of our exploration lies a comprehensive understanding of sustainable business practices. We unravel the intricacies of what it means for a business to be sustainable, examining the economic, social, and environmental dimensions. By defining these practices, we set the stage for a transformative journey towards resilient and responsible business operations.

Importance of Long-Term Success in Business

Beyond immediate gains, the significance of long-term success cannot be overstated. We delve

into why businesses must extend their horizon
beyond quarterly profits and consider enduring
success. By exploring the advantages of
sustainability in fostering longevity, resilience, and
positive impact, we lay the groundwork for a
strategic shift in business thinking.

As we progress through the chapters, we navigate
the Triple Bottom Line—balancing economic,
social, and environmental sustainability. From
financial responsibility and ethical investments to
employee well-being and community engagement,
each facet is dissected to provide practical insights.

The journey continues by examining how
sustainability can be seamlessly integrated into
day-to-day operations. From responsible supply
chain management to energy efficiency, we unveil
strategies for businesses to adopt and thrive in an era
where sustainability is not just a buzzword but a
fundamental business imperative.

Building a sustainable culture becomes our focal
point in the subsequent chapters, exploring the
pivotal role of leadership commitment, employee

engagement, and transparent communication in shaping an organization's ethos.

Sustainable innovation takes center stage as we explore how businesses can proactively contribute to a greener future through research and development, eco-friendly product design, and circular economy practices.

Our exploration then shifts towards the crucial aspect of measuring and reporting sustainability, essential for businesses to track progress, adhere to standards, and effectively communicate their efforts to stakeholders.

Inevitably, challenges emerge in any transformative journey. We confront issues like resistance to change, financial constraints, and regulatory compliance, providing pragmatic approaches to overcome these hurdles.

Through illuminating case studies, we draw inspiration from successful companies embracing sustainable practices and glean valuable lessons from failures, offering a holistic view of the landscape.

WHAT IS SUSTAINABLE BUSINESS PRACTICES.

Sustainable business practices refer to a set of ethical, socially responsible, and environmentally conscious strategies employed by organizations to balance profit generation with long-term societal and environmental well-being. These practices extend beyond traditional business goals, emphasizing a commitment to economic viability, social equity, and environmental stewardship. Companies engaging in sustainable business practices seek to minimize their negative impact on the planet, promote ethical business conduct, and contribute positively to the communities in which they operate. This holistic approach aims to create enduring value, foster resilience, and align business objectives with the broader goals of sustainable development. Embracing sustainable business practices is not only a moral imperative but increasingly recognized as a strategic necessity in a world where environmental and social challenges demand thoughtful and responsible corporate action.

CHAPTER TWO.

THE TRIPLE BOTTOM LINE

A. ECONOMIC SUSTAINABILITY

1. Financial Responsibility.

In the realm of economic sustainability, financial responsibility stands as the bedrock for a business's long-term viability. We explore the principles of sound financial management, emphasizing prudent budgeting, strategic investment, and the cultivation of financial resilience. Understanding the delicate balance between profitability and responsibility, we delve into practices that safeguard economic health without compromising ethical integrity. Financial responsibility is a cornerstone of sustainable business practices, embodying the conscientious management of financial resources to ensure long-term viability, stability, and ethical integrity. This facet of sustainability extends beyond profit generation, emphasizing the prudent allocation of funds, transparency in financial dealings, and a commitment to ethical financial practices. Here's an in-depth exploration of financial responsibility within the context of sustainable business practices:

a. Prudent Budgeting: Sustainable financial management begins with a meticulous budgeting process. Businesses need to allocate resources efficiently, balancing operational needs with long-term financial goals. Prudent budgeting involves forecasting, strategic planning, and a keen understanding of the organization's financial landscape. This ensures that financial decisions align with overall sustainability objectives and contribute to the business's enduring success.

b. Strategic Investment: Financial responsibility goes hand in hand with strategic investment. Rather than focusing solely on short-term gains, businesses committed to financial responsibility evaluate investments based on their long-term impact. This may involve considering the environmental and social consequences of investments, ensuring alignment with the company's values and sustainability goals. Strategic investments contribute not only to financial growth but also to the overall resilience and sustainability of the business.

c. Risk Management: Financial responsibility requires a proactive approach to risk management. Businesses need to identify, assess, and mitigate financial risks to safeguard their long-term interests. This includes considerations of market fluctuations, regulatory changes, and other external factors that may impact financial stability. By developing robust risk management strategies, businesses can navigate uncertainties and maintain financial responsibility in dynamic business environments.

d. Ethical Financial Practices: Upholding ethical standards in financial dealings is a fundamental aspect of financial responsibility. This encompasses fair and transparent financial reporting, honest communication with stakeholders, and adherence to legal and regulatory requirements. Ethical financial practices not only build trust among stakeholders but also contribute to the overall reputation of the business as a responsible corporate citizen.

e.   Long-Term Sustainability: Financial responsibility is intrinsically linked to the long-term sustainability of a business. By making financially sound decisions and considering the broader impacts of financial activities, businesses can position themselves for enduring success. This involves aligning financial strategies with environmental, social, and governance (ESG) principles, reflecting a commitment to responsible and sustainable business practices.

In conclusion, financial responsibility is not just a financial metric; it's a guiding principle that shapes the ethos of a sustainable business. Businesses that prioritize financial responsibility contribute not only to their own resilience but also to the broader goals of creating a sustainable and responsible business environment.

2. Ethical Investment.

Beyond profitability, businesses are increasingly recognizing the power of ethical investments. This section unveils the concept of ethical investment and its role in fostering sustainable business practices. From socially responsible investments to environmentally conscious financial decisions, we navigate the landscape of aligning financial strategies with values, ensuring that economic success is intertwined with ethical considerations. Ethical investment, also known as socially responsible investment (SRI) or sustainable investment, is a financial strategy that goes beyond mere profit considerations to incorporate ethical, social, and environmental factors into investment decisions. This approach aligns investors' values with their financial goals, seeking to generate returns while supporting businesses that demonstrate responsible and sustainable practices. Here's an in-depth exploration of ethical investment:

I.   Alignment with Values: At the core of ethical investment is the alignment of financial decisions with personal or institutional values. Investors actively seek opportunities that reflect their ethical principles, whether those involve environmental stewardship, social justice, human rights, or other sustainability considerations. This alignment ensures that the investment portfolio is a reflection of the investor's commitment to making a positive impact beyond financial returns.

II. Environmental, Social, and Governance (ESG) Criteria: Ethical investment involves a thorough evaluation of potential investments based on ESG criteria. These criteria assess a company's performance in environmental sustainability, social responsibility, and corporate governance. Investors consider factors such as a company's carbon footprint, treatment of employees, diversity and inclusion policies, ethical sourcing, and overall corporate transparency. By integrating ESG criteria, ethical investors aim to support businesses that prioritize sustainability and responsible practices.

III. Negative and Positive Screening: Ethical investment employs screening processes to either exclude certain industries or companies (negative screening) or actively include those that meet specific ethical criteria (positive screening). Negative screening may involve avoiding investments in industries such as tobacco, weapons, or fossil fuels, while positive screening seeks out companies with outstanding ESG practices and positive societal impacts.

IV. Impact Investing: Impact investing is a subset of ethical investment that specifically focuses on generating positive social or environmental impacts alongside financial returns. Investors actively seek projects or companies that contribute to solutions for global challenges, such as climate change, poverty alleviation, or healthcare access. Impact investing aims to be a force for positive change, leveraging financial resources to address pressing societal and environmental issues.

V. Community Development: Ethical investors often prioritize community development as a

key criterion for investment. This involves
supporting businesses that engage in fair
labor practices, contribute to local economies,
and foster positive relationships with the
communities in which they operate. Ethical
investors recognize the interconnectedness of
business success and community well-being.

VI.   Transparency and Reporting: Transparency is
a fundamental aspect of ethical investment.
Companies that embrace ethical practices are
expected to provide transparent and
comprehensive reporting on their ESG
performance. Ethical investors value clear
communication about a company's impact on
the environment, its treatment of employees,
and its overall commitment to ethical
business conduct.

VII.   Global Standards and Certification: Ethical
investment often involves adherence to global
standards and certifications, such as the
United Nations Principles for Responsible
Investment (UN PRI) or various sustainable
finance certifications. These standards
provide a framework for ethical investors to

assess and compare the sustainability
performance of different investment options.

In conclusion, ethical investment represents a paradigm shift in the financial world, acknowledging that financial success can and should coexist with ethical, social, and environmental responsibility. As more investors recognize the importance of aligning their portfolios with their values, ethical investment continues to gain prominence as a powerful force for positive change in the global economy.

B. <u>SOCIAL SUSTAINABILITY</u>

1. Employee Well-being:

The heartbeat of any organization is its workforce. We shine a spotlight on the pivotal role of employee well-being in the pursuit of social sustainability. From fostering a positive workplace culture to implementing wellness programs, we explore how businesses can prioritize the health and happiness of their employees. Recognizing that engaged and satisfied employees are key drivers of long-term success, we provide actionable insights for creating workplaces that nurture both personal and professional growth. Employee well-being is a holistic concept that goes beyond physical health to encompass various aspects of an individual's life within and outside the workplace. Recognizing that employees are a company's most valuable asset, prioritizing their well-being is not only a moral imperative but also a strategic investment in organizational success. Here's a comprehensive exploration of the different dimensions of employee well-being:

1. Physical Health:
   Physical well-being forms the foundation of employee health. Companies that prioritize physical well-being provide resources and support for maintaining a healthy lifestyle. This may include wellness programs, access to fitness facilities, health screenings, and initiatives promoting healthy nutrition. A focus on physical health contributes to increased energy levels, reduced absenteeism, and improved overall productivity.

2. Mental Health:

Acknowledging the importance of mental health is crucial in fostering a supportive workplace. Employee assistance programs, mental health days, and access to counseling services are increasingly common offerings. Creating a stigma-free environment where employees feel comfortable discussing mental health concerns contributes to a positive workplace culture and can lead to increased job satisfaction and engagement.

3. Work-Life Balance:

Striking a balance between work and personal life is essential for employee well-being. Companies that promote flexible work hours, remote work options, and reasonable expectations regarding workload contribute to a healthier work-life balance. This not only reduces stress but also enhances job satisfaction and overall happiness.

4. Career Development Opportunities:

Supporting employees' professional growth is a key component of well-being. Providing access to training, mentorship programs, and opportunities for career advancement fosters a sense of purpose and fulfillment. Employees who feel invested in their professional development are more likely to be engaged and committed to the organization.

5. Inclusive and Diverse Culture:
   Employee well-being is closely linked to the culture of the workplace. Cultivating an inclusive and diverse environment where every employee feels valued and respected contributes to a positive sense of well-being. Companies that prioritize diversity and inclusion not only create a more vibrant workplace but also benefit from a variety of perspectives and ideas.

6. Recognition and Appreciation:
   Feeling valued is integral to employee well-being. Recognition programs, regular feedback, and expressions of appreciation contribute to a positive work environment. Recognized employees tend to be more motivated, satisfied, and committed to their roles.

7. Safe and Healthy Work Environment:
   Physical safety within the workplace is a fundamental aspect of employee well-being. Companies need to ensure that workplaces are free from hazards, comply with safety regulations, and

provide appropriate training to minimize the risk of accidents. A safe and healthy work environment contributes to employee morale and overall well-being.

8. Financial Wellness Programs:
   Financial stress can significantly impact employee well-being. Companies that offer financial wellness programs, including educational resources, assistance with budgeting, and retirement planning support, help alleviate financial concerns and contribute to a more secure and satisfied workforce.

9. Social Connection and Team Building:
   Building strong social connections among employees fosters a sense of community. Team-building activities, social events, and open communication channels contribute to a positive workplace culture. Socially connected employees are more likely to collaborate effectively and experience a higher level of job satisfaction.

In conclusion, employee well-being is a multifaceted concept that requires a comprehensive and integrated approach. Companies that prioritize the physical, mental, and professional health of their employees not only create a positive workplace culture but also position themselves for increased productivity, innovation, and long-term success.

2. Community Engagement:

Businesses don't exist in isolation; they are integral parts of communities. This section underscores the importance of community engagement as a cornerstone of social sustainability. We delve into strategies for businesses to actively contribute to the well-being of the communities they operate in. Whether through philanthropy, volunteer initiatives, or collaborative projects, we explore avenues for businesses to build meaningful connections and be positive contributors to the social fabric. Community engagement is a strategic and proactive approach that organizations adopt to build meaningful relationships with the communities in which they operate. It goes beyond philanthropy, emphasizing collaboration, communication, and shared responsibility. Successful community engagement not only benefits local communities but also enhances a company's reputation, strengthens stakeholder relationships, and contributes to long-term sustainability. Here's a comprehensive exploration of community engagement:

I.   Understanding Local Needs: The foundation of effective community engagement is a thorough understanding of the needs and concerns of the local community. Companies engage in dialogue with community members, local authorities, and other stakeholders to identify key issues, challenges, and opportunities. This understanding forms the basis for targeted and impactful community initiatives.

II.   Stakeholder Collaboration: Community engagement involves collaboration with various stakeholders, including local residents, non-profit organizations, government agencies, and other businesses. By working together, organizations can leverage collective expertise and resources to address community challenges and create positive change.

III. Corporate Social Responsibility (CSR) Programs: CSR programs are a common avenue for community engagement. These initiatives involve the allocation of resources, such as financial support, employee volunteering, and in-kind donations, to address social and environmental issues. CSR activities are designed to align with community needs and contribute to the overall well-being of the local population.

IV. Skills and Capacity Building: Community engagement goes beyond providing financial support. Companies actively contribute to the capacity-building of local communities by offering skills development programs, training sessions, and educational initiatives. Empowering community members with the skills and knowledge they need enhances their self-sufficiency and resilience.

V. Environmental Stewardship: Businesses engage with local communities on environmental initiatives to mitigate their impact on the environment. This may include initiatives such as tree planting, waste

reduction programs, and water conservation
efforts. Engaging communities in
environmental stewardship not only benefits
the local ecosystem but also strengthens the
bond between the company and the
community.

VI.   Cultural Respect and Sensitivity: Successful
community engagement requires cultural
respect and sensitivity. Companies must be
aware of and respect the cultural norms,
traditions, and values of the communities
they interact with. Building trust through
cultural understanding is essential for the
success of community engagement initiatives.

VII.   Community-Informed Decision-Making:
Inclusion of community perspectives in
decision-making processes is a hallmark of
effective community engagement. Businesses
seek input from local residents on matters
that may impact the community, ensuring that
decisions are made with a comprehensive
understanding of the community's needs and
aspirations.

VIII.   Open Communication Channels:
Transparency and open communication are
fundamental to community engagement.
Companies establish clear channels of
communication with the community,
providing updates on projects, seeking
feedback, and addressing concerns. Regular
and open communication fosters trust and
strengthens the relationship between the
organization and the community.

IX.   Long-Term Commitment: Genuine
community engagement requires a long-term
commitment. Companies recognize that
sustainable positive impact takes time, and
ongoing efforts are necessary to address
evolving community needs. Long-term
commitment builds a legacy of trust and
collaboration.

X.   Measuring Impact and Reporting: Effective
community engagement involves measuring
the impact of initiatives and transparently
reporting the outcomes. This accountability
ensures that community resources are used

effectively and that the organization remains committed to making a positive difference.

In conclusion, community engagement is a dynamic and reciprocal relationship between businesses and the communities they serve. By actively participating in and contributing to community well-being, organizations not only fulfill their social responsibilities but also foster a positive reputation, enhance stakeholder relationships, and contribute to the overall sustainability of both the business and the community.

C. ENVIRONMENTAL SUSTAINABILITY

1. Resource Efficiency.

Resource efficiency is not just an environmental concern; it's a strategic imperative. This part of the chapter delves into practices that optimize resource utilization, reduce waste, and enhance overall efficiency. From adopting circular economy principles to embracing sustainable sourcing, businesses can harness resource efficiency to not only reduce their environmental impact but also enhance their operational effectiveness. Resource efficiency is a strategic approach that emphasizes the responsible and sustainable use of resources to minimize waste, reduce environmental impact, and enhance overall operational effectiveness. This concept extends across various sectors, including businesses, industries, and public institutions, recognizing that optimizing resource utilization is crucial for long-term sustainability. Resource efficiency involves maximizing the value derived from available resources while minimizing waste and environmental impact. It encompasses a comprehensive understanding of resource inputs, production processes, and the sustainable use of materials, energy, and other inputs.

- Sustainable Sourcing:

Sustainable sourcing is a key aspect of resource efficiency. Companies aim to procure materials and resources from responsibly managed sources. This involves evaluating the environmental and social impact of suppliers, ensuring ethical practices throughout the supply chain, and supporting sustainable extraction or production methods.

- Circular Economy Principles:

Resource efficiency aligns closely with the principles of a circular economy. Instead of the traditional linear "take-make-dispose" model, a circular economy emphasizes reducing, reusing, and recycling resources. Businesses adopting circular economy principles design products with longevity in mind, promote recycling initiatives, and seek ways to close the loop on material flows.

- Waste Reduction Strategies:

Efficient resource use involves minimizing waste generation. Businesses implement waste reduction strategies, including optimizing production processes, reusing materials, and implementing recycling programs. By reducing waste, companies not only contribute to environmental sustainability but also enhance operational efficiency.

- Energy Efficiency:

Energy is a critical resource, and optimizing its use is central to resource efficiency. Companies adopt energy-efficient technologies, implement conservation measures, and explore the adoption of renewable energy sources. Energy efficiency initiatives contribute to cost savings, reduce carbon emissions, and enhance overall operational sustainability.

- Water Conservation:

Resource efficiency extends to water usage, particularly in regions facing water scarcity. Companies implement water conservation measures, such as efficient irrigation systems, wastewater recycling, and responsible water management practices, to minimize the environmental impact and ensure the sustainable use of this essential resource.

- Life Cycle Assessment (LCA):

Life Cycle Assessment is a methodology employed to evaluate the environmental impact of products or processes throughout their entire life cycle. By conducting LCAs, businesses gain insights into the resource use, emissions, and environmental consequences associated with their operations, enabling informed decisions to enhance resource efficiency.

- Technology and Innovation:

Embracing technological advancements and fostering innovation is crucial for resource efficiency. Businesses invest in technologies that optimize processes, reduce resource consumption, and enhance overall efficiency. Innovations such as smart manufacturing, IoT (Internet of Things), and sustainable materials contribute to resource-efficient practices.

- Regulatory Compliance:

Governments and regulatory bodies often play a role in promoting resource efficiency through legislation and standards. Businesses align with and adhere to these regulations, ensuring that their operations meet or exceed required standards for resource use and environmental impact.

- Supply Chain Optimization

Resource efficiency extends beyond individual companies to their entire supply chains. Businesses work collaboratively with suppliers and partners to optimize resource use collectively. This involves joint initiatives to reduce waste, enhance energy efficiency, and promote sustainable practices throughout the supply chain.

In conclusion, resource efficiency is a fundamental pillar of sustainable business practices. By optimizing resource use, companies not only contribute to environmental conservation but also enhance their resilience, reduce operational costs, and align with the evolving expectations of environmentally conscious consumers and stakeholders.

2. Carbon Footprint Reduction.

As the global community grapples with climate change, businesses play a crucial role in mitigating their carbon footprint. We explore practical approaches for businesses to measure, manage, and ultimately reduce their carbon emissions. From energy-efficient practices to embracing renewable energy sources, this section provides a roadmap for businesses to contribute to environmental sustainability while enhancing their brand reputation and future-proofing their operations. Carbon footprint reduction is a critical component of sustainable business practices aimed at mitigating climate change and minimizing the environmental impact of human activities, particularly the emission of greenhouse gasses, primarily carbon dioxide. Businesses adopting carbon footprint reduction strategies acknowledge their role in addressing climate change and work towards minimizing their carbon emissions. Here's a comprehensive exploration of carbon footprint reduction:

The carbon footprint represents the total amount of greenhouse gasses, measured in carbon dioxide equivalents (CO2e), emitted directly or indirectly by an individual, organization, event, or product throughout its lifecycle. Understanding and quantifying this footprint is the first step in devising effective reduction strategies.

1. Energy Efficiency Measures:

Energy consumption is a significant contributor to carbon emissions. Businesses implement energy efficiency measures, such as adopting energy-efficient technologies, optimizing building systems, and promoting responsible energy use. This not only reduces carbon emissions but also often leads to cost savings.

2. Renewable Energy Adoption:

Transitioning to renewable energy sources, such as solar, wind, and hydropower, is a key strategy for carbon footprint reduction. By replacing or supplementing traditional energy sources with renewables, businesses can significantly decrease their reliance on fossil fuels and reduce carbon emissions associated with energy production.

3. Carbon Offsetting:
Carbon offsetting involves investing in projects or initiatives that remove or reduce an equivalent amount of greenhouse gasses elsewhere. This can include supporting reforestation efforts, investing in renewable energy projects, or participating in carbon capture and storage initiatives. Carbon offsetting complements direct emission reduction efforts.

4. Sustainable Transportation:
Businesses address carbon emissions associated with transportation by promoting sustainable alternatives. This may involve using electric or hybrid vehicles, encouraging public transportation or carpooling, and investing in logistics strategies that optimize transportation routes to minimize emissions.

5. Supply Chain Optimization:
The carbon footprint extends throughout the entire supply chain. Businesses work collaboratively with suppliers to identify and implement carbon reduction initiatives. This may include selecting

suppliers with environmentally friendly practices, optimizing transportation logistics, and promoting sustainable sourcing.

6. Energy-Efficient Buildings:
Designing and retrofitting buildings to meet energy efficiency standards is crucial for carbon footprint reduction. Improved insulation, energy-efficient lighting, and smart building systems contribute to reducing the energy demand of facilities, thereby lowering carbon emissions.

7. Waste Management and Recycling:
Proper waste management and recycling efforts reduce the carbon emissions associated with the disposal of materials. By implementing effective waste reduction strategies, businesses contribute to a circular economy, minimizing the need for new raw materials and decreasing the overall carbon impact of their operations.

8. Employee Engagement:
Engaging employees in carbon reduction initiatives fosters a culture of sustainability within the organization. Businesses educate employees on the importance of carbon footprint reduction,

encourage sustainable practices in the workplace, and involve staff in identifying and implementing innovative solutions.

9. Lifecycle Assessments:

Conducting life cycle assessments (LCAs) helps businesses identify the carbon impact of products or processes at every stage, from raw material extraction to disposal. This comprehensive analysis informs decision-making, enabling companies to prioritize areas for carbon footprint reduction.

In conclusion, carbon footprint reduction is a multifaceted approach that requires a commitment to sustainability across various aspects of business operations. By adopting strategies that focus on energy efficiency, renewable energy adoption, sustainable transportation, and supply chain optimization, businesses contribute to global efforts to address climate change while simultaneously enhancing their long-term resilience and reputation.

CHAPTER THREE.

INTEGRATING SUSTAINABILITY INTO OPERATIONS

A. SUPPLY CHAIN MANAGEMENT

Supply Chain Management (SCM) is a systematic and strategic approach to the end-to-end coordination of the processes involved in the production and distribution of goods and services. It encompasses the planning, sourcing, manufacturing, logistics, and delivery processes, aiming to optimize efficiency, reduce costs, and enhance overall competitiveness. Here's a comprehensive exploration of supply chain management:

Key Components of Supply Chain Management.

01. Planning: Forecasting demand, setting production schedules, and aligning resources to meet anticipated demand.

02. Sourcing: Identifying and selecting suppliers, negotiating contracts, and managing relationships with vendors.
03. Manufacturing or Production: Transforming raw materials into finished goods through efficient and cost-effective processes.
04. Logistics: Coordinating the movement of goods, including transportation, warehousing, and distribution.
05. Delivery or Fulfillment: Ensuring products reach customers in a timely and efficient manner.

Supplier Relationship Management.

Building strong and collaborative relationships with suppliers is crucial for a resilient supply chain. This involves effective communication, transparent information sharing, and the establishment of mutual trust. Strong supplier relationships contribute to better reliability, quality, and responsiveness in the supply chain.

Risk Management.

Identifying and mitigating risks is an integral part of supply chain management. This includes assessing potential disruptions such as natural disasters, geopolitical issues, or changes in market demand. Developing risk mitigation strategies ensures the continuity of operations even in the face of unforeseen challenges.

I. Technology Integration:

Leveraging technology is essential for modern supply chain management. Technologies such as RFID (Radio-Frequency Identification), IoT (Internet of Things), and advanced analytics enable real-time visibility, data-driven decision-making, and enhanced overall efficiency.

II. Inventory Management:

Efficient inventory management is critical for balancing supply and demand. Businesses aim to minimize excess inventory while ensuring products are available when needed. Just-in-time (JIT) and lean inventory practices are commonly employed to optimize stock levels.

III. Lean Supply Chain:

The lean supply chain philosophy focuses on minimizing waste and maximizing efficiency. It involves streamlining processes, reducing excess inventory, and improving overall agility. Adopting

lean principles enhances responsiveness to changes
in demand and market dynamics.

IV.   Sustainability in Supply Chains:
  Sustainable supply chain practices involve
considering environmental, social, and ethical
factors. This includes sustainable sourcing, reducing
the carbon footprint, promoting fair labor practices,
and adopting eco-friendly packaging. Sustainable
supply chain management aligns with corporate
social responsibility and meets the expectations of
environmentally conscious consumers.

V.   Collaborative Planning, Forecasting, and
       Replenishment (CPFR):
  CPFR is a collaborative approach where trading
partners share information to enhance forecasting
accuracy, reduce stockouts, and optimize inventory
levels. This collaborative planning fosters better
communication and coordination throughout the
supply chain.

VI.   Continuous Improvement:
  Supply chain management is an evolving
discipline that requires a commitment to continuous
improvement. Regularly assessing performance,

identifying areas for optimization, and adapting to changes in the business environment are essential for a resilient and effective supply chain.

In conclusion, effective supply chain management is a cornerstone for business success, influencing both operational efficiency and customer satisfaction. By adopting a holistic approach that integrates planning, sourcing, manufacturing, logistics, and delivery processes, businesses can optimize their supply chain, reduce costs, and navigate the complexities of the global marketplace. Supply Chain Management involves the seamless integration and coordination of various activities, entities, and resources to deliver products or services to end consumers. It extends beyond the boundaries of individual organizations and includes suppliers, manufacturers, distributors, retailers, and customers.

1. Sustainable Sourcing.

The backbone of any sustainable business lies in its supply chain. We delve into the importance of sustainable sourcing, exploring how businesses can make conscientious choices in procuring materials and resources. From evaluating the environmental impact of suppliers to ensuring ethical labor practices, this section provides insights into fostering a supply chain that aligns with sustainability goals. Sustainable sourcing not only mitigates environmental harm but also enhances brand reputation and builds stronger relationships with suppliers who share a commitment to responsible practices.

2. Fair Trade Practices.

Fair trade goes beyond mere transactions; it embodies a commitment to social justice. We unravel the significance of fair trade practices within supply chain management. By ensuring fair wages, safe working conditions, and equitable treatment of workers, businesses can contribute to social sustainability. This section navigates the principles and benefits of fair trade, illustrating how businesses can integrate these practices into their supply chain, fostering positive impacts on both local and global communities.

B. ENERGY EFFICIENCY

Energy efficiency is a key strategy for optimizing the use of energy resources to achieve maximum output while minimizing waste and environmental impact. It involves adopting technologies, practices, and policies that enhance the performance of energy systems, reduce consumption, and promote sustainability. Energy efficiency also contributes to cost savings, resource conservation, and increased overall sustainability. Here's a comprehensive exploration of energy efficiency:

Energy Efficiency in Buildings.
01. Building Design: Incorporating energy-efficient design principles in construction, such as proper insulation, orientation, and the use of energy-efficient materials.
02. Appliances and Lighting: Adopting energy-efficient appliances, lighting systems, and HVAC (heating, ventilation, and air conditioning) technologies to reduce electricity consumption.
03. Smart Building Systems: Implementing smart building technologies that optimize energy usage through automation and data-driven decision-making.

Industrial Energy Efficiency.

01. Process Optimization: Streamlining industrial processes to reduce energy waste and improve overall efficiency.
02. Energy Audits: Conducting energy audits to identify areas for improvement and implementing energy-saving measures in manufacturing and production facilities.
03. Advanced Technologies: Adopting advanced technologies, such as energy-efficient motors, variable-speed drives, and waste heat recovery systems, to enhance industrial energy efficiency.

Transportation Energy Efficiency.
01. Fuel Efficiency: Promoting fuel-efficient vehicles and optimizing transportation routes to reduce fuel consumption.
02. Alternative Fuels: Exploring and adopting alternative fuels, such as electric, hydrogen, or biofuels, to reduce the environmental impact of transportation.
03. Public Transportation: Encouraging the use of public transportation and implementing policies that support sustainable mobility solutions.

Renewable Energy Integration.

01. Solar and Wind Power: Harnessing renewable energy sources, such as solar and wind power, to generate electricity with minimal environmental impact.

02. Hydropower: Utilizing hydropower as a clean and efficient energy source for electricity generation.

03. Energy Storage: Implementing energy storage solutions, such as batteries, to store excess energy generated by renewables for later use.

Information Technology (IT) Energy Efficiency.

01. Data Center Efficiency: Implementing energy-efficient practices in data centers, including efficient cooling systems, server virtualization, and energy-efficient hardware.

02. Electronic Devices: Designing and manufacturing energy-efficient electronic devices, promoting energy-saving features, and encouraging responsible disposal practices.

Government Policies and Standards.

01. Energy Efficiency Standards: Governments often establish energy efficiency standards for

appliances, vehicles, and industrial processes
to encourage the adoption of energy-efficient
technologies.

02. Incentive Programs: Offering financial
incentives and subsidies to businesses and
individuals adopting energy-efficient
practices.

03. Building Codes: Enforcing building codes
that incorporate energy-efficient design and
construction practices.

Consumer Awareness and Behavior.

01. Education: Raising awareness among
consumers about the importance of energy
efficiency and providing information on
energy-saving practices.

02. Energy Conservation Habits: Encouraging
individuals to adopt energy-saving habits,
such as turning off lights, using
energy-efficient appliances, and reducing
overall energy consumption.

International Cooperation.

01. Global Agreements: Participating in
international agreements and initiatives

focused on promoting energy efficiency and reducing global energy consumption.

02. Knowledge Sharing: Sharing best practices and technological advancements globally to accelerate the adoption of energy-efficient solutions.

Monitoring and Measurement.

01. Energy Audits: Conducting regular energy audits to assess energy consumption, identify inefficiencies, and implement targeted improvements.

02. Key Performance Indicators (KPIs): Establishing and monitoring KPIs related to energy efficiency to track progress and drive continuous improvement.

In conclusion, energy efficiency is a multifaceted approach that involves collaboration between individuals, businesses, governments, and international organizations. By embracing energy-efficient technologies, adopting sustainable practices, and implementing supportive policies, societies can achieve significant reductions in energy consumption, mitigate environmental impacts, and move towards a more sustainable and resilient energy future.

Energy efficiency refers to the ability to achieve desired outcomes with the least amount of energy input. It plays a crucial role in addressing environmental concerns, such as climate change, by reducing greenhouse gas emissions associated with energy production and consumption.

1. Renewable Energy Adoption.

In the pursuit of environmental sustainability, the adoption of renewable energy sources stands as a pivotal step. We explore the various forms of renewable energy, from solar and wind to geothermal, and their integration into business operations. Transitioning to renewable energy not only reduces a company's carbon footprint but also positions it as a leader in the global shift towards sustainable practices. Practical insights and case studies demonstrate how businesses can navigate this transformative journey, reaping both environmental and economic benefits. Renewable energy adoption involves transitioning from traditional fossil fuel-based energy sources to cleaner, sustainable alternatives derived from naturally replenishing resources. This transition is driven by the need to address environmental challenges, reduce greenhouse gas emissions, and create a more sustainable and resilient energy future. Here's a comprehensive exploration of renewable energy adoption:

Types of Renewable Energy.
01. Solar Energy: Harnessing energy from the sun through photovoltaic cells to generate electricity or through solar thermal systems for heating.
02. Wind Energy: Capturing the kinetic energy of the wind through wind turbines to generate electricity.
03. Hydropower: Utilizing the energy of flowing or falling water to generate electricity through turbines.
04. Biomass Energy: Using organic materials, such as wood, agricultural residues, or organic waste, to produce heat or generate electricity.
05. Geothermal Energy: Tapping into the Earth's internal heat for heating, electricity generation, or direct use applications.

Environmental Benefits.

01. Reduced Greenhouse Gas Emissions: Renewable energy sources produce electricity with significantly lower greenhouse gas emissions compared to fossil fuels, helping mitigate climate change.

02. Air and Water Pollution Reduction: Unlike fossil fuel combustion, renewable energy technologies generally have lower environmental impacts, reducing air and water pollution.

Economic Advantages.

01. Job Creation: The renewable energy sector creates jobs in manufacturing, installation, maintenance, and research, contributing to economic growth.

02. Cost Competitiveness: Advances in technology have made many renewable energy sources increasingly cost-competitive with traditional energy sources, leading to reduced electricity costs.

Technological Innovations.

01. Advancements in Solar Technology: Improvements in solar panel efficiency,

reduced costs, and innovations in solar
storage technologies have driven widespread
solar energy adoption.
02. Smart Grids: Integrating renewable energy
sources into smart grids enables efficient
electricity distribution, load balancing, and
integration of diverse energy sources.

Government Incentives and Policies.
01. Renewable Portfolio Standards (RPS):
Mandates requiring a percentage of energy to
come from renewable sources, encouraging
utilities to adopt clean energy.
02. Feed-In Tariffs: Providing financial
incentives for individuals or businesses that
generate renewable energy and feed it back
into the grid.
03. Tax Credits and Subsidies: Governments
often offer tax credits and subsidies to
incentivize the adoption of renewable energy
technologies.

Community and Residential Adoption.
01. Residential Solar Panels: The installation of
solar panels on residential rooftops allows
homeowners to generate their own clean

energy and potentially sell excess electricity
back to the grid.

02. Community Solar Projects: Shared solar
installations enable communities to
collectively benefit from solar energy
generation, particularly for those unable to
install individual systems.

2. Waste Reduction Strategies.

Waste is not just a byproduct; it's an opportunity
for innovation. This section delves into strategies for
businesses to minimize waste generation and move
towards a circular economy. From implementing
recycling programs to designing products with
end-of-life considerations, we explore how waste
reduction strategies can enhance operational
efficiency and contribute to environmental
sustainability. By embracing a "reduce, reuse,
recycle" ethos, businesses can align their operations
with the principles of sustainability while creating a
positive impact on the planet.

Waste reduction strategies are approaches and
initiatives aimed at minimizing the generation of
waste, promoting responsible consumption, and

fostering a circular economy where resources are used efficiently. These strategies contribute to environmental sustainability, reduce the strain on landfills, and minimize the overall ecological impact of waste disposal. Here's a comprehensive exploration of waste reduction strategies:

Source Reduction.
01. Product Design: Designing products with minimal packaging, using recyclable materials, and ensuring longevity to reduce the need for frequent replacements.
02. Bulk Purchasing: Encouraging consumers to buy in bulk, reducing individual packaging and overall waste generated.

Reuse and Repurposing.
01. Promoting Reusable Items: Encouraging the use of reusable items such as shopping bags, water bottles, and containers to reduce reliance on single-use disposable products.
02. Community Swap Events: Organizing events where individuals can exchange or donate items they no longer need, promoting reuse within the community.

Recycling Programs.
   01. Education and Awareness: Raising awareness
       about the importance of recycling and
       providing information on what materials are
       recyclable.
   02. Waste Separation: Implementing effective
       waste separation programs to ensure that
       recyclable materials are diverted from
       landfills.

Composting.
   01. Composting Facilities: Establishing
       community or municipal composting
       facilities to process organic waste into
       nutrient-rich compost.
   02. Home Composting: Encouraging individuals
       to compost at home, reducing the amount of
       organic waste sent to landfills.

Waste-to-Energy Technologies.
   01. Incineration: Implementing controlled waste
       incineration processes that convert waste into
       energy, reducing the volume of waste and
       generating electricity.
   02. Anaerobic Digestion: Using anaerobic
       digestion to break down organic waste,

producing biogas for energy and nutrient-rich byproducts.

Extended Producer Responsibility (EPR).

01. Product Take-Back Programs: Implementing EPR policies that require manufacturers to take responsibility for the disposal of their products, encouraging recycling and responsible end-of-life management.
02. Design for Disassembly: Encouraging manufacturers to design products with components that can be easily disassembled for recycling or reuse.

Circular Economy Practices.

01. Closed-Loop Systems: Adopting circular economy principles, where products are designed to be reused, refurbished, or recycled, reducing the need for new raw materials.
02. Product Life Extension: Promoting practices that extend the lifespan of products through repair, refurbishment, or upgrading.

Reducing Food Waste.

01. Educational Campaigns: Educating consumers about meal planning, proper food storage, and understanding expiration dates to reduce food waste.
02. Donations to Food Banks: Encouraging businesses to donate surplus food to food banks or community organizations instead of discarding it.

How Purchasing Policies: Implementing procurement policies that prioritize environmentally friendly products with minimal packaging and a commitment to sustainability.
Supplier Engagement: Engaging with suppliers to encourage sustainable and responsible packaging practices.

Legislation and Regulation.
01. Waste Reduction Laws: Enacting and enforcing laws that regulate waste generation, encourage recycling, and hold businesses

accountable for responsible waste
management.
02. Plastic Bans and Restrictions: Implementing
restrictions on single-use plastics and
promoting alternatives to reduce plastic
waste.

Consumer Education and Engagement.

Campaigns and Workshops: Conducting
educational campaigns and workshops to inform the
public about waste reduction strategies, responsible
consumption, and the environmental impact of
waste.

Technology Innovation.
01. Waste Sorting Technologies: Investing in
advanced technologies for automated waste
sorting to enhance the efficiency of recycling
processes.
02. Biodegradable Materials: Encouraging the
development and use of biodegradable
materials as alternatives to traditional,
non-biodegradable products.

In conclusion, waste reduction strategies encompass a broad range of approaches, from individual behavioral changes to systemic shifts in production and consumption patterns. By adopting these strategies, communities, businesses, and governments contribute to a more sustainable and circular economy, where resources are used efficiently, and the environmental impact of waste is minimized.

CHAPTER FOUR.

BUILDING A SUSTAINABLE CULTURE.

Leadership commitment is a foundational element for the successful implementation of sustainable business practices. When leaders are dedicated to integrating sustainability into the core values and operations of an organization, it sets the tone for a culture that prioritizes environmental and social responsibility. Here's a comprehensive exploration of leadership commitment in the context of sustainable business practices:

Visionary Leadership.

Leaders play a crucial role in shaping the vision for sustainability within an organization. A visionary leader communicates a compelling and clear vision that aligns sustainability goals with the overall mission and values of the company.

Incorporating Sustainability into Strategy.

Effective leaders ensure that sustainability is integrated into the strategic planning process. This involves aligning sustainability objectives with the overall business strategy, making it an integral part of decision-making at all levels of the organization.

Resource Allocation.

Leadership commitment is reflected in the allocation of resources, both financial and human, to support sustainable initiatives. This includes budgetary allocations for sustainability programs, hiring dedicated personnel, and investing in sustainable technologies and practices.

Setting Targets and Metrics.

Leaders establish clear and measurable sustainability targets. By defining key performance indicators (KPIs), leaders provide a framework for assessing progress and holding the organization accountable for its sustainability commitments.

Lead by Example.

Leading by example is a powerful form of commitment. When leaders actively engage in sustainable practices, such as reducing their own carbon footprint or participating in community initiatives, it reinforces the importance of sustainability throughout the organization.

Stakeholder Engagement.
Engaging with stakeholders, including employees, customers, investors, and the broader community, demonstrates leadership commitment. Leaders seek input, listen to concerns, and transparently communicate the organization's sustainability efforts.

Integration with Corporate Culture.
Commitment to sustainability becomes ingrained in the corporate culture under strong leadership. Leaders foster a culture where sustainable practices are not viewed as an isolated initiative but as an integral part of how the organization operates.

Continuous Learning.
Leaders exhibit a commitment to continuous learning and adaptation. Given the dynamic nature of sustainability challenges, leaders stay informed about emerging trends, technologies, and best

practices, ensuring the organization remains at the forefront of sustainable innovation.

Advocacy and Influence.

Leaders leverage their positions to advocate for sustainable policies at both internal and external levels. This can involve influencing industry standards, engaging in policy discussions, and advocating for sustainability on a broader scale.

Risk Management.

Leaders recognize the potential risks associated with environmental, social, and governance (ESG) factors. By incorporating sustainability into risk management strategies, they proactively address challenges and enhance the organization's resilience.

Long-Term Perspective.

Leadership commitment to sustainability often entails adopting a long-term perspective. Instead of focusing solely on short-term gains, leaders understand the importance of sustainable practices for the organization's longevity and resilience in a changing business landscape.

Recognition and Rewards.

Leaders implement systems for recognizing and rewarding individuals and teams that contribute significantly to the organization's sustainability goals. This encourages a positive feedback loop and reinforces the value placed on sustainable efforts.

In conclusion, leadership commitment is fundamental to the success of sustainable business practices. It sets the foundation for organizational culture, influences strategic decisions, and demonstrates to stakeholders that sustainability is not merely a trend but a core value. Organizations with dedicated leaders committed to sustainability are better positioned to navigate the complexities of the modern business environment while contributing positively to societal and environmental well-being.

A. <u>EMPLOYEE TRAINING AND ENGAGEMENT.</u>

Employee training and engagement are critical components of building a sustainable culture within an organization. When employees are educated about sustainability principles and feel empowered to contribute to environmental and social responsibility, it fosters a sense of collective responsibility and enhances the organization's overall commitment to sustainability. Here's a comprehensive exploration of employee training and engagement in the context of sustainable business practices:

1.   Educational Programs.
Implementing comprehensive educational programs that educate employees about sustainability concepts, the organization's sustainability goals, and the broader environmental and social impact of their work.

2.   Skill Development.
Offering training programs that equip employees with the skills necessary to contribute effectively to sustainable initiatives. This may include specific job-related skills, such as green product design, sustainable supply chain management, or energy-efficient practices.

3.   Empowering Employees.

Encouraging a sense of ownership and empowerment among employees by creating an environment where individuals feel they can contribute innovative ideas and take actions that positively impact the organization's sustainability performance.

4.   Incorporating Sustainability into Onboarding
Integrating sustainability education into the onboarding process for new employees. This ensures that sustainability is introduced as a core value from the beginning of an employee's journey with the organization.

5.   Cross-Functional Collaboration.
Facilitating cross-functional collaboration through training initiatives. This allows employees from various departments to work together on sustainability projects, fostering a holistic and integrated approach to sustainability.

6.   Recognition and Rewards.
Recognizing and rewarding employees for their contributions to sustainability goals. Acknowledging achievements, whether through formal recognition programs, awards, or incentives, creates a positive

feedback loop and reinforces the importance of sustainable efforts.

7.   Communication Channels.
Establishing effective communication channels for employees to share insights, concerns, and innovative ideas related to sustainable practices. Open dialogue ensures that employees feel heard and engaged in the organization's sustainability journey.

8.   Goal Alignment.
Aligning individual and team goals with sustainability objectives. When employees understand how their work contributes to broader sustainability goals, it enhances their sense of purpose and connection to the organization's mission.

9.   Performance Reviews.
Incorporating sustainability performance into employee performance reviews. Linking sustainability contributions to performance evaluations reinforces the organization's commitment to sustainability as a core aspect of individual and team success.

10.   Continuous Learning Opportunities.

Providing continuous learning opportunities to keep employees informed about evolving sustainability trends, emerging technologies, and best practices. This ensures that employees remain knowledgeable and adaptable in the rapidly changing sustainability landscape.

11.   Employee Resource Groups.

Establishing employee resource groups or committees focused on sustainability. These groups can serve as forums for employees to share ideas, collaborate on initiatives, and drive sustainability efforts within the organization.

12.   Community Engagement.

Encouraging employees to participate in community engagement activities related to sustainability. This involvement not only extends the organization's impact beyond the workplace but also strengthens employees' sense of purpose and community connection.

13.   Flexible Learning Formats.

Offering flexible learning formats, such as online courses, workshops, and seminars, to accommodate diverse learning styles and preferences among employees.

14.   Feedback Mechanisms.
Implementing feedback mechanisms that allow employees to provide input on sustainability programs and initiatives. Actively seeking and incorporating employee feedback demonstrates a commitment to inclusivity and continuous improvement.

In conclusion, employee training and engagement are integral to cultivating a sustainable culture within organizations. By providing education, empowering employees, and recognizing their contributions, organizations create a workforce that is not only environmentally conscious but also actively involved in driving positive change. Employee engagement in sustainability initiatives contributes to a sense of shared responsibility and aligns individual efforts with the organization's commitment to long-term environmental and social impact.

B. <u>TRANSPARENT COMMUNICATION.</u>

Transparent communication is a cornerstone of building a sustainable culture within an organization. When leaders and employees communicate openly and honestly about sustainability initiatives, goals, and progress, it fosters trust, accountability, and a shared commitment to environmental and social responsibility. Here's a comprehensive exploration of transparent communication in the context of sustainable business practices:

1. Open Dialogue.

Establishing and encouraging open dialogue about sustainability efforts within the organization. Leaders create an environment where employees feel comfortable sharing ideas, concerns, and feedback related to sustainability.

2. Stakeholder Engagement.

Engaging with external stakeholders, including customers, suppliers, investors, and the broader community, through transparent communication. This involves sharing information about the organization's sustainability practices, performance, and future goals.

3. Reporting and Disclosure.
Regularly reporting on sustainability performance and progress toward goals. Transparent disclosure, whether through sustainability reports, websites, or other channels, allows stakeholders to assess the organization's commitment and impact.

4. Setting Realistic Expectations.
Clearly articulating realistic expectations regarding sustainability goals and initiatives. Transparent communication ensures that stakeholders have a clear understanding of what the organization aims to achieve and the steps being taken to reach those goals.

5. Addressing Challenges Honestly.
Acknowledging challenges and setbacks openly. Transparent communication involves admitting when things don't go as planned and demonstrating a commitment to learning and improvement.

6. Two-Way Communication.
Establishing two-way communication channels that allow for feedback and input from all levels of the organization. Leaders actively listen to

employees' ideas and concerns, creating a culture of collaboration and inclusivity.

7. Accessibility of Information.

Ensuring that information related to sustainability is easily accessible to all stakeholders. This includes making reports, data, and updates available through various channels, such as company websites, intranets, and public forums.

8. Consistent Messaging.

Maintaining consistency in messaging across various communication platforms. Transparent communication requires alignment in the way sustainability information is presented internally and externally to avoid confusion or mixed signals.

9. Celebrating Successes.

Transparent communication involves not only addressing challenges but also celebrating successes openly. Recognizing achievements, whether big or small, reinforces the positive impact of sustainability efforts and motivates stakeholders.

10. Educational Campaigns.

Conducting educational campaigns to inform stakeholders about the importance of sustainability, the organization's goals, and the impact of their collective efforts. Education fosters understanding and support for sustainable initiatives.

11. Crisis Communication.

Establishing a transparent approach to crisis communication related to sustainability issues. Leaders communicate promptly and honestly in times of crisis, addressing concerns and outlining corrective actions being taken.

12. Feedback Loops.

Implementing feedback loops that allow stakeholders to provide input on sustainability initiatives. Actively seeking and incorporating feedback demonstrates a commitment to continuous improvement and responsiveness to stakeholder concerns.

13. Employee Communication Channels.

Utilizing various communication channels, including newsletters, town hall meetings, and internal forums, to keep employees informed about sustainability initiatives, progress, and upcoming plans.

14. Accessibility to Leadership.
Ensuring accessibility to leadership for questions and discussions related to sustainability. Transparent communication involves making leaders approachable and available for dialogue.

15. Data Transparency.
Providing transparent access to relevant sustainability data and metrics. This includes sharing key performance indicators (KPIs) and metrics that demonstrate the organization's environmental and social impact.

In conclusion, transparent communication is an essential element in the successful implementation of sustainable business practices. Organizations that prioritize openness and honesty in their communication about sustainability not only build trust with stakeholders but also create a culture of accountability and shared responsibility. Transparent communication is a dynamic process that evolves with the organization's sustainability journey, fostering a resilient and positive impact on both internal and external stakeholders.

CHAPTER FIVE.

SUSTAINABLE INNOVATION.

In the ever-evolving landscape of business, sustainable innovation stands as a cornerstone for long-term success. Sustainable innovation refers to the process of developing and implementing new ideas, products, services, or business practices that have positive environmental, social, and economic impacts over the long term. It involves finding creative solutions to address challenges related to sustainability, such as environmental degradation, resource depletion, and social inequality.

Key aspects of sustainable innovation include:

I. Environmental Responsibility:
Prioritizing the use of eco-friendly materials, reducing carbon emissions, and minimizing waste in the development of products or services. Environmental responsibility refers to the ethical obligation of individuals, organizations, and communities to act in ways that minimize negative impacts on the environment and promote sustainable

practices. It involves a conscious effort to protect and preserve the natural world, considering the finite resources available and the interconnectedness of ecosystems.

Key components of environmental responsibility include:

1) Conservation of Resources: Using natural resources efficiently and avoiding unnecessary waste. This includes minimizing energy consumption, reducing water usage, and responsibly managing raw materials.

2) Pollution Prevention: Taking measures to prevent and reduce pollution. This involves minimizing emissions, properly disposing of waste, and adopting practices that reduce environmental contamination.

3) Biodiversity Preservation: Recognizing the importance of biodiversity and working to protect and restore ecosystems. This includes efforts to conserve wildlife, protect natural habitats, and promote sustainable land use.

4) Carbon Footprint Reduction: Implementing strategies to reduce greenhouse gas emissions, both in daily activities and in industrial processes. This can involve transitioning to renewable energy sources, improving energy efficiency, and supporting carbon offset initiatives.

5) Compliance with Environmental Regulations: Adhering to local, national, and international environmental laws and regulations. This ensures that activities are conducted within established guidelines to prevent harm to the environment.

6) Education and Advocacy: Promoting awareness and understanding of environmental issues within communities and encouraging responsible behavior. Advocacy efforts may involve supporting policies that address environmental challenges.

7) Sustainable Practices: Embracing sustainable business practices, such as eco-friendly product design, adopting circular economy principles, and integrating environmentally conscious policies into day-to-day operations.

Environmental responsibility is a critical aspect of corporate social responsibility and individual citizenship. By embracing environmentally responsible practices, individuals and organizations contribute to the broader goal of creating a more sustainable and resilient planet for current and future generations.

II. Social Impact.

Considering the well-being of communities, workers, and society at large in innovation efforts, ensuring fair labor practices and promoting inclusivity. Social impact refers to the effect or influence that actions, initiatives, or policies have on the well-being and development of society. It encompasses the positive changes, improvements, or challenges experienced by individuals, communities, or the broader population as a result of certain activities. Social impact can be intentional, as seen in philanthropic efforts or community development projects, or unintentional, arising from various business practices, policies, or technological advancements.

Key aspects of social impact include:

1. Positive Outcomes: Social impact is often associated with positive outcomes that contribute to the betterment of society. This can include improved access to education, healthcare, housing, and employment opportunities.

2. Addressing Social Issues: Initiatives or interventions that aim to address and mitigate social challenges such as poverty, inequality, discrimination, and social injustice contribute positively to social impact.

3. Community Engagement: Involving and empowering communities in decision-making processes and development initiatives fosters a sense of ownership and ensures that interventions are aligned with local needs and priorities.

4. Environmental and Ethical Considerations: Social impact extends beyond direct social outcomes and may include considerations for environmental sustainability and ethical

practices. Businesses, for example, can have a positive social impact by adopting environmentally responsible and ethical business practices.

5. Measurable Change: Social impact is often measured by tangible changes in social indicators, such as improved quality of life, increased access to essential services, or enhanced social inclusion.

6. Corporate Social Responsibility (CSR): Many businesses actively pursue social impact through their CSR initiatives, which involve actions and policies that contribute positively to society, beyond their core business activities.

Understanding and assessing social impact is essential for organizations, policymakers, and individuals aiming to make meaningful and positive contributions to the well-being of society. It involves a comprehensive evaluation of the intended and unintended consequences of actions, as well as a commitment to continuous improvement in addressing social challenges.

III. Economic Viability.

 Balancing sustainability with economic considerations to create solutions that are financially feasible and contribute to long-term business success. Economic viability refers to the ability of a project, business, or initiative to be sustainable and profitable over the long term. It involves assessing whether the financial aspects of a venture are sound enough to support its ongoing operations, growth, and success. Economic viability goes beyond short-term profitability and considers the overall health and resilience of an economic endeavor.

Key components of economic viability include:

1. Profitability: The project or business must generate profits, ensuring that revenues exceed costs. A sustainable level of profitability is crucial for continued operations and future investments.

2. Cost Management: Efficient management of costs is essential for economic viability. This includes controlling operational expenses, optimizing

resource utilization, and implementing cost-saving measures.

3. Market Demand: A viable economic initiative aligns with market demand. Understanding and responding to customer needs, preferences, and trends is vital for sustained success in a competitive environment.

4. Risk Management: Assessing and mitigating risks is a key element of economic viability. This involves identifying potential challenges, implementing risk management strategies, and maintaining flexibility to adapt to changing economic conditions.

5. Return on Investment (ROI): Evaluating the return on investment is critical for determining economic viability. This involves analyzing the financial returns relative to the capital invested, providing insights into the project's overall financial performance.

6. Cash Flow Management: Maintaining positive cash flow is crucial for economic viability. Businesses must ensure that they have sufficient

liquidity to cover operating expenses, debt
obligations, and unforeseen contingencies.

7. Adaptability to Economic Conditions: Economic
viability requires the ability to adapt to changing
economic conditions, regulatory environments, and
market dynamics. This adaptability enhances
resilience and long-term success.

8. Ethical and Legal Considerations: Operating
within ethical and legal frameworks is essential for
economic viability. Compliance with regulations and
ethical business practices builds trust with
stakeholders and minimizes the risk of legal issues.

Ensuring economic viability is fundamental for the
sustained growth and success of businesses and
projects. Striking a balance between financial
performance, market alignment, and risk
management contributes to the overall resilience and
longevity of economic endeavors.

IV. Life Cycle Thinking.

Evaluating the entire life cycle of a product or service, from raw material extraction to disposal, to minimize negative impacts on the environment. Life Cycle Thinking is an approach that considers the entire life cycle of a product, process, or service, from its creation to its end-of-life disposal or recycling. It involves assessing the environmental, social, and economic aspects at each stage of the life cycle to make informed and sustainable decisions.

Key elements of Life Cycle Thinking include:

1. Raw Material Acquisition: Evaluating the environmental and social impacts associated with extracting and processing raw materials for the production of a product.

2. Manufacturing and Production: Assessing the energy consumption, emissions, and waste generated during the manufacturing process, as well as the social aspects such as labor conditions.

3. Distribution and Transportation: Analyzing the environmental and economic impacts of transporting

and distributing the product to consumers, considering factors like energy use, emissions, and transportation efficiency.

4. Product Use: Understanding the environmental and social implications during the use phase, including energy consumption, emissions, and the potential for product maintenance or repairs.

5. End-of-Life Management: Evaluating the disposal or recycling phase, considering the environmental impact of waste generation and the potential for recycling or reuse. This phase also includes assessing the social aspects of waste management.

Life Cycle Thinking aims to minimize the negative impacts associated with each stage of a product's life cycle while maximizing positive contributions. It provides a holistic perspective that goes beyond focusing solely on manufacturing or product use and encourages a more sustainable approach to design, production, and consumption.
By adopting Life Cycle Thinking, businesses and individuals can make more informed decisions to reduce environmental impact, improve resource

efficiency, and promote overall sustainability throughout the life cycle of products and services.

V. Collaboration.

Engaging in partnerships and collaborations with stakeholders, including customers, suppliers, and communities, to enhance the effectiveness and acceptance of sustainable innovations. Collaboration is the process of individuals or entities working together to achieve a common goal or objective. It involves sharing ideas, resources, and efforts to achieve a mutually beneficial outcome. Collaboration can occur in various settings, including businesses, academic institutions, community projects, and more.

Key aspects of collaboration include:

1. Shared Goals: Collaborators come together with a shared purpose or objective. Clear and common goals provide a foundation for collective effort and synergy.

2. Communication: Effective communication is crucial in collaboration. Open and transparent communication ensures that all parties involved are on the same page, leading to better understanding and coordination.

3. Mutual Benefit: Collaboration is often driven by the recognition that working together can yield benefits for all involved parties. This mutual benefit can be in the form of shared resources, expertise, or the accomplishment of shared goals.

4. Teamwork: Collaboration involves individuals working as a team, pooling their skills, knowledge, and efforts to achieve a collective outcome. It fosters a sense of unity and shared responsibility.

5. Flexibility: Successful collaboration requires flexibility and adaptability. Participants may need to adjust their approaches, perspectives, or timelines to accommodate the needs of the collaborative effort.

6. Respect and Trust: Building trust and mutual respect among collaborators is essential. Trust is the foundation for effective communication and cooperation.

7. Diversity and Inclusion: Collaboration often benefits from diverse perspectives and skills. Inclusive collaboration values the contributions of individuals from different backgrounds, experiences, and expertise.

8. Conflict Resolution: Conflicts may arise in collaborative efforts. Effective collaboration involves addressing conflicts constructively and finding resolutions that support the overall goals of the collaboration.

Whether in professional settings, community projects, or research endeavors, collaboration harnesses the collective power of individuals to achieve outcomes that may be challenging or impossible to attain independently. It is a dynamic process that promotes innovation, creativity, and shared success.

Sustainable innovation is also crucial for businesses seeking to adapt to changing global priorities, meet consumer expectations, and contribute positively to the planet and society. It represents a shift towards a more responsible and resilient approach to business and development.

A. <u>RESEARCH AND DEVELOPMENT FOR SUSTAINABILITY</u>.

In the pursuit of sustainable business practices, a commitment to Research and Development (R&D) plays a central role. This involves a proactive approach to understanding environmental challenges and developing innovative solutions. Companies should allocate resources to explore technologies, materials, and methodologies that minimize their ecological footprint.

1. Environmental Impact Assessment: Begin by conducting a comprehensive assessment of your business's environmental impact. This includes analyzing resource usage, waste generation, and overall carbon footprint. Identifying key areas for improvement will guide your R&D initiatives.

2. Investment in Green Technologies: Allocate funds to research and adopt green technologies that enhance energy efficiency, reduce waste, and lower emissions.

Collaborate with experts and leverage external partnerships to stay at the forefront of sustainable advancements.

3. Integration of Circular Economy Principles: Embrace the principles of a circular economy by designing products with a lifecycle approach. R&D efforts should focus on creating products that can be easily recycled, repurposed, or refurbished, minimizing waste and promoting a sustainable product lifecycle.

B. ECO-FRIENDLY PRODUCT DESIGN.

A fundamental aspect of sustainable business practices lies in the way products are designed. Eco-friendly product design not only aligns with environmental ethics but also caters to a growing consumer demand for responsible and sustainable choices.

1. Life Cycle Assessment: Incorporate Life Cycle Assessment (LCA) methodologies into product design. Assess the environmental impact of each stage, from raw material extraction to manufacturing, distribution, and

disposal. This holistic approach ensures a thorough understanding of a product's ecological footprint.

2. Material Selection: Choose materials with lower environmental impact. Prioritize recyclable or biodegradable materials, and consider alternatives that reduce reliance on scarce resources. Additionally, explore sustainable sourcing practices to support ethical supply chains.

3. Energy-Efficient Design: Implement energy-efficient design principles to minimize energy consumption during the manufacturing and usage phases. This includes optimizing processes, utilizing renewable energy sources, and designing products with energy conservation in mind.

By integrating these elements into your business model, sustainable innovation becomes a catalyst for long-term success. Research and Development for Sustainability, coupled with Eco-friendly Product Design, not only aligns your business with environmental responsibility but also positions it as a leader in a world where sustainable practices are paramount for a thriving future.

C. <u>CIRCULAR ECONOMY PRACTICES</u>.
Circular Economy Practices aim to shift from the traditional linear model of "take, make, dispose" to a more sustainable approach. Key elements include recycling, reusing, and reducing waste. Designing products for longevity, promoting repairability, and encouraging responsible consumption contribute to a closed-loop system, minimizing environmental impact. This approach fosters resource efficiency and helps build a more sustainable and resilient economy. They are also an holistic approach to resource management and waste reduction, seeking to create a sustainable, closed-loop system. Several key strategies contribute to this:

1. Design for Longevity:
   - Products are designed with durability in mind, ensuring a longer lifespan.
   - Emphasis on high-quality materials and construction to withstand wear and tear.

2. Reuse and Repair:
- Encouraging the reuse of products through refurbishment, remanufacturing, or repurposing.
- Promoting repairability by providing spare parts and repair services, extending the life of goods.

3. Recycling:
- Efficient recycling processes to recover materials from end-of-life products.
- Closed-loop recycling systems aim to reintroduce recycled materials into new products.

4. Waste Reduction:
- Minimizing waste generation through efficient production processes.
- Implementing practices like source reduction and lean manufacturing to cut down on unnecessary waste.

5. Resource Efficiency:
- Optimal use of resources, focusing on reducing raw material extraction and consumption.

- Adopting technologies that enhance resource productivity and efficiency.

6. Product as a Service (PaaS):
   - Shifting from ownership to service models where consumers lease or rent products.
   - Manufacturers retain responsibility for product maintenance, repair, and end-of-life disposal.

7. Digital Technologies:
   - Utilizing technologies like the Internet of Things (IoT) for better product tracking and maintenance.
   - Smart design principles enhance resource management and reduce environmental impact.

8. Collaboration and Innovation:
   - Fostering collaboration among industries, policymakers, and consumers to create a supportive ecosystem.
   - Encouraging innovation in materials, production processes, and business models.

9. Consumer Awareness:
  - Educating consumers about sustainable consumption habits.
  - Encouraging conscious buying decisions and responsible disposal practices.

10. Regulatory Support:
  - Implementing policies and regulations that incentivize circular economy practices.
  - Providing frameworks to hold businesses accountable for their environmental impact.

Circular Economy Practices not only contribute to environmental sustainability but also offer economic benefits by reducing resource dependence and creating new business opportunities. As global awareness of environmental issues grows, the adoption of circular economy principles becomes crucial for building a resilient and sustainable future.

CHAPTER SIX.

MEASURING AND REPORTING SUSTAINABILITY.

In the pursuit of long-term success through sustainable business practices, measuring and reporting sustainability becomes a cornerstone. This chapter explores the critical elements of this process, delving into Key Performance Indicators (KPIs), Sustainability Reporting Standards, and the importance of effective Stakeholder Communication.

A. <u>KEY PERFORMANCE INDICATORS (KPIs).</u>
Key Performance Indicators (KPIs) are measurable values that organizations use to evaluate their success in achieving specific objectives. These indicators are crucial in assessing the performance of various aspects of a business, providing insights into how well goals are being met. KPIs can cover a wide range of areas, including financial

performance, customer satisfaction, operational efficiency, and, importantly, sustainability.

In the context of sustainability, KPIs help measure and track environmental, social, and economic performance. For instance:

Environmental KPIs.

Environmental Key Performance Indicators (KPIs) are metrics used to assess and measure an organization's environmental performance and impact. These indicators focus on various aspects related to resource use, energy consumption, emissions, and other environmental aspects. Monitoring and improving environmental KPIs are crucial for businesses committed to sustainability and responsible environmental stewardship.

Common Environmental KPIs include:

1. Carbon Emissions: Measures the total amount of greenhouse gas emissions produced by the organization, often expressed as carbon dioxide equivalents (CO2e).

2. Energy Consumption: Evaluates the amount
   of energy used by the organization, including
   electricity, gas, and other forms of energy.

3. Water Usage: Tracks the amount of water
   consumed by the organization in its
   operations.

4. Waste Generation: Measures the total amount
   of waste produced by the organization,
   distinguishing between recyclable,
   compostable, and non-recyclable waste.

5. Renewable Energy Adoption: Indicates the
   percentage of energy obtained from
   renewable sources, such as solar or wind
   power.

6. Biodiversity Impact: Assesses the impact of
   business activities on local ecosystems and
   biodiversity.

7. Resource Efficiency: Evaluates how efficiently resources (raw materials, energy, etc.) are used in the production process.

8. Product Life Cycle Analysis: Analyzes the environmental impact of a product throughout its life cycle, from raw material extraction to disposal.

9. Eco-friendly Product Development: Measures the proportion of products developed with environmentally friendly materials and processes.

10. Environmental Compliance: Ensures adherence to environmental regulations and standards.

11. Sustainable Supply Chain: Evaluates the sustainability practices of suppliers and the overall environmental impact of the supply chain.

12. Eco-efficient Processes: Assesses the efficiency of production processes in minimizing environmental impact.

By tracking and improving environmental KPIs, organizations can mitigate their ecological footprint, promote resource conservation, and contribute to a more sustainable and resilient future. Integrating these environmental indicators with economic and social KPIs provides a comprehensive view of a company's triple bottom line performance.

Social KPIs.

Social Key Performance Indicators (KPIs) are metrics used to assess and measure an organization's social performance and impact. These indicators focus on various aspects related to the well-being of employees, relationships with communities, and the broader social impact of the business. Social KPIs are crucial for evaluating a company's commitment to corporate social responsibility (CSR) and its contributions to social sustainability.

Common Social KPIs include:

1. Employee Satisfaction and Engagement: Measures the overall satisfaction of

employees and their level of engagement
with their work.

2. Diversity and Inclusion Metrics: Evaluates
the representation of diverse groups within
the workforce, including gender, ethnicity,
and other demographic factors.

3. Health and Safety Performance: Monitors
workplace safety records, incident rates, and
the effectiveness of health and safety
programs.

4. Training and Development: Assesses the
investment in employee training and
development programs to enhance skills and
knowledge.

5. Employee Well-being: Measures initiatives
and policies supporting the physical and
mental well-being of employees.

6. Community Impact: Examines the positive
contributions an organization makes to the
communities in which it operates.

7. Philanthropy and Charitable Contributions: Quantifies financial support and resources provided to charitable causes and community projects.

8. Human Rights Compliance: Ensures adherence to human rights standards throughout the supply chain and business operations.

9. Supplier Diversity: Assesses the inclusion of diverse suppliers and vendors in the supply chain.

10. Social License to Operate: Measures the acceptance and support of the company by the communities and stakeholders in its operational areas.

11. Employee Volunteering and Community Involvement: Tracks the participation of employees in volunteer activities and community outreach programs.

Monitoring and improving social KPIs demonstrate a company's commitment to ethical business practices, fostering a positive corporate culture, and contributing to the well-being of society. Integrating social KPIs with economic and environmental indicators provides a holistic view of a company's triple bottom line performance.

Economic KPIs

Economic Key Performance Indicators (KPIs) are metrics used to assess and measure the financial performance and economic health of an organization. These indicators provide valuable insights into various aspects of a company's financial well-being and help stakeholders, including management, investors, and analysts, understand the overall economic sustainability of the business.

Common Economic KPIs include:

1. Revenue Growth: Measures the increase in total sales over a specific period, indicating the company's ability to generate income.

2. Profit Margins: Examines the percentage of profit earned relative to revenue, revealing how efficiently the company is converting sales into profits.

3. Return on Investment (ROI): Evaluates the profitability of an investment by comparing the return to the cost of the investment.

4. Operating Income: Represents the profit generated from regular business operations before interest and taxes.

5. Cash Flow: Assesses the amount of cash moving in and out of the business, indicating its liquidity and ability to meet financial obligations.

6. Debt-to-Equity Ratio: Examines the proportion of debt to equity, providing insights into the company's financial leverage and risk.

7. Cost of Goods Sold (COGS): Measures the direct costs associated with producing goods or services, influencing profit margins.

8. Working Capital: Evaluates the company's short-term liquidity by subtracting current liabilities from current assets.

9. Earnings Before Interest, Taxes, Depreciation, and Amortization (EBITDA): Represents the company's operating performance by excluding non-operating expenses.

10. Customer Lifetime Value (CLV): Estimates the total value a customer brings to the company over their entire relationship, aiding in customer-focused economic analysis.

Economic KPIs play a crucial role in strategic decision-making, financial planning, and performance evaluation. For businesses committed to sustainability, integrating economic KPIs with environmental and social indicators provides a comprehensive view of their overall impact and performance.By establishing and monitoring relevant KPIs, organizations can make informed decisions, track progress, and demonstrate their commitment to sustainability to stakeholders.

- Evaluating financial performance through sustainable revenue streams.

- Monitoring investments in innovation, cost reductions, and overall economic resilience.

B. <u>SUSTAINABILITY REPORTING STANDARDS.</u>

Sustainability Reporting Standards are frameworks and guidelines that organizations follow to disclose their environmental, social, and economic performance in a structured and standardized manner. These standards provide a common language and set of principles for businesses to communicate their sustainability efforts transparently to stakeholders, including investors, customers, employees, and the public.

Several prominent sustainability reporting standards exist, and organizations often choose the one that aligns best with their industry, goals, and stakeholders. Here are some well-known frameworks:

1. Global Reporting Initiative (GRI): A widely used framework providing comprehensive guidelines for reporting on economic,

environmental, and social dimensions. GRI
Standards are designed to be adaptable to
various sectors and industries.

2. Sustainability Accounting Standards Board
    (SASB): Focuses on industry-specific
    standards, providing a set of disclosure
    recommendations tailored to the unique
    sustainability issues relevant to different
    sectors.

3. Integrated Reporting Framework: Encourages
    organizations to present a holistic view of
    their performance by integrating financial and
    non-financial information into a single,
    cohesive report.

4. Task Force on Climate-related Financial
    Disclosures (TCFD): Offers
    recommendations for disclosing
    climate-related risks and opportunities in
    financial filings, ensuring transparency about
    the impact of climate change on business
    operations.

5. Carbon Disclosure Project (CDP): Known for its focus on climate-related disclosures, CDP provides a platform for companies to report on their environmental impact, particularly related to carbon emissions and climate risks.

6. ISO 26000: An international standard offering guidance on social responsibility, providing principles and core subjects for organizations to consider in their sustainability efforts.

Adhering to sustainability reporting standards helps organizations:
- Enhance transparency and accountability.
- Facilitate comparisons and benchmarking with industry peers.
- Build trust with stakeholders by providing a standardized and reliable set of information.
- Demonstrate commitment to sustainable and responsible business practices.

These standards contribute to the growing emphasis on corporate responsibility and sustainability, enabling stakeholders to make informed decisions and encouraging businesses to integrate sustainable practices into their core operations.

C. <u>STAKEHOLDER COMMUNICATION.</u>
Stakeholder communication refers to the exchange of information and engagement activities between an organization and its stakeholders. Stakeholders are individuals or groups that have an interest, influence, or are affected by the organization's activities and decisions. Effective communication with stakeholders is crucial for building trust, managing expectations, and fostering positive relationships.

Key aspects of stakeholder communication include:

1. Identification of Stakeholders: Recognizing and understanding the various individuals, groups, or entities that have a stake in or are impacted by the organization's actions.

2. Engagement Strategies: Developing tailored approaches to involve stakeholders in decision-making processes, seeking their input, feedback, and collaboration.

3. Transparent Communication: Providing clear, honest, and timely information about the organization's activities, performance, and future plans.

4. Two-Way Communication: Encouraging an open dialogue where stakeholders can express their concerns, ask questions, and provide insights.

5. Tailored Messaging: Customizing communication strategies to address the specific interests, needs, and concerns of different stakeholder groups.

6. Regular Updates: Keeping stakeholders informed through regular updates, reports, newsletters, or other communication channels.

7. Handling Feedback: Acknowledging and addressing feedback from stakeholders, demonstrating responsiveness to their concerns.

8. Crisis Communication: Establishing protocols for communicating with stakeholders during crises or challenging situations, ensuring transparency and managing reputational risks.

9. Technology and Social Media Integration:
Leveraging technology and social media platforms
to reach a wide audience and engage with
stakeholders in real-time.

10. Sustainability Reporting: Communicating the
organization's sustainability efforts, performance,
and impact on environmental, social, and economic
aspects.

Effective stakeholder communication is vital for
organizations committed to sustainable practices, as
it helps align business objectives with stakeholder
expectations. Whether it's employees, customers,
investors, local communities, or regulatory bodies,
clear and consistent communication fosters a shared
understanding of the organization's values and
contributes to long-term success.

In conclusion, the journey towards sustainable
business practices requires a robust framework for
measuring, reporting, and communicating efforts.
By implementing effective KPIs, adhering to
recognized reporting standards, and fostering
transparent stakeholder communication, businesses

can not only enhance their reputation but also contribute to a more sustainable and resilient future. This chapter serves as a guide for navigating the intricacies of sustainability metrics and ensuring that the impact of sustainable practices is accurately conveyed to all stakeholders.

CHAPTER SEVEN.

OVERCOMING CHALLENGES IN SUSTAINABLE BUSINESS PRACTICES.

Embarking on the journey of sustainable business practices is not without its hurdles. This chapter explores key challenges faced by organizations and strategies to overcome them, focusing on Resistance to Change, Financial Constraints, and Regulatory Compliance.

A. RESISTANCE TO CHANGE.

Resistance to change refers to the reluctance or opposition that individuals or groups within an organization may exhibit when faced with alterations to established processes, structures, or routines. This resistance can manifest in various forms and can hinder the successful implementation of new initiatives, strategies, or practices.

Common reasons for resistance to change include:

1. Fear of the Unknown:
The fear of the unknown is a common human emotion characterized by anxiety or uneasiness about uncertain situations, outcomes, or unfamiliar experiences. It is a natural response to situations where individuals lack clear information or predictability, leading to a sense of insecurity or apprehension.

Key aspects of the fear of the unknown include:

01. Uncertainty: The fear often arises when facing situations with unpredictable outcomes, creating a sense of vulnerability due to the lack of clarity.
02. Change and Transition: Transitions or significant changes in life, whether personal or professional, can trigger fear of the unknown as individuals grapple with the unfamiliar.
03. Risk Perception: Perceived risks associated with the unknown, such as potential negative

outcomes or consequences, contribute to heightened anxiety.
04. Imagination and Anticipation:The imagination tends to fill gaps in information, and anticipation of what might happen amplifies feelings of fear.
05. Loss of Control: Feeling a lack of control over a situation or the inability to influence outcomes can intensify the fear of the unknown.

Overcoming the fear of the unknown often involves:

01. Information and Understanding: Seeking information and understanding about the unknown can help alleviate fear. Knowledge empowers individuals to make informed decisions.
02. Mindfulness and Present Moment Awareness: Practicing mindfulness and focusing on the present moment can help individuals manage anxiety associated with an uncertain future.
03. Positive Framing: Shifting perspective by focusing on potential positive outcomes and

viewing the unknown as an opportunity for growth and learning.

04. Gradual Exposure: Gradually exposing oneself to new experiences or situations can help desensitize the fear and build confidence over time.

05. Support System: Having a supportive network of friends, family, or colleagues can provide encouragement and reassurance during uncertain times.

Recognizing that the fear of the unknown is a common and natural emotion can be the first step in managing it effectively. Embracing uncertainty as a part of life's journey and approaching it with a positive mindset can lead to personal growth and resilience.

2. Loss of Control:

The fear of loss of control is an emotional response characterized by anxiety or discomfort related to the perceived inability to influence or manage certain aspects of one's life or circumstances. This fear often arises when individuals feel that events or situations are beyond their control, leading to a sense of powerlessness.

Key aspects of the fear of loss of control include:

01. Uncertainty: The fear intensifies in situations where outcomes are uncertain, and individuals cannot predict or influence the course of events.

02. Change: Transitions, unexpected changes, or disruptions can trigger a fear of losing control, as individuals grapple with adapting to new circumstances.

03. Dependency on External Factors: Feeling dependent on external factors or relying on others for decisions can contribute to the fear of losing control over one's life.

04. Vulnerability: The perception of vulnerability, where individuals believe they have little protection or defense against negative outcomes, amplifies the fear.

05. Coping Mechanisms: Some individuals may use rigid routines or obsessive behaviors as coping mechanisms to maintain a sense of control, and disruptions to these routines can heighten anxiety.

Overcoming the fear of loss of control involves various strategies:

01. Mindfulness: Practicing mindfulness techniques, such as meditation or deep breathing, can help individuals stay present and manage anxiety related to uncontrollable factors.

02. Focus on the Present: Concentrating on what can be controlled in the present moment rather than worrying about the future helps individuals regain a sense of stability.

03. Acceptance: Embracing the idea that not everything can be controlled and accepting uncertainty as a natural part of life can reduce fear.

04. Adaptive Coping Strategies: Developing adaptive coping strategies, such as problem-solving skills and flexibility, enables individuals to navigate challenges effectively.

05. Seeking Support: Engaging with a support system, whether through friends, family, or professional counseling, provides emotional support and guidance during uncertain times.

06. Setting Realistic Expectations: Recognizing and setting realistic expectations about the controllable aspects of life helps individuals focus on achievable goals and reduce anxiety.

Understanding that complete control is often an illusion and learning to navigate life's uncertainties can contribute to a healthier mindset. While certain aspects may be beyond control, individuals have the capacity to adapt, make choices, and cultivate resilience in the face of change and unpredictability.

3. Comfort with the Status Quo:
Comfort with the status quo refers to an individual's or an organization's inclination to maintain existing conditions, routines, or practices without actively seeking or embracing change. It is a state of being content or at ease with the current state of affairs, and it can have both positive and negative implications.

Key Aspects of Comfort with the Status Quo:

01. Familiarity: People may prefer the status quo because it is familiar, known, and requires less effort to navigate.
02. Risk Aversion: A reluctance to change can stem from a fear of the unknown or the perceived risks associated with embracing something new.
03. Routine and Stability: Comfort with the status quo often aligns with a desire for stability, predictability, and established routines.
04. Resistance to Disruption: Individuals or organizations comfortable with the status quo may resist disruptions to established norms, processes, or ways of doing things.

Positive Aspects:

01. Stability and Consistency: Comfort with the status quo can provide stability and consistency, creating a sense of security and predictability.

02. Efficiency: Established routines and processes may lead to increased efficiency, as individuals become adept at navigating familiar tasks.

03. Reduced Anxiety: Avoiding frequent changes may contribute to lower stress levels, as individuals know what to expect in their daily lives or work environments.

Negative Aspects:

01. Innovation Stagnation: Over Reliance on the status quo can hinder innovation and the exploration of new ideas or approaches

02. Missed Opportunities: Resisting change may lead to missing out on potential opportunities for growth, improvement, or advancement.

03. Lack of Adaptability: Comfort with the status quo may result in a lack of adaptability to changing circumstances or evolving market dynamics.

Balancing Comfort with the Need for Change:

01. Assessment of Impact: Regularly assessing the impact of the status quo on personal or organizational goals helps determine whether change is necessary for growth and success.
02. Openness to Innovation: Encouraging an open mindset and a willingness to embrace innovation can help break away from excessive comfort with the status quo.
03. Continuous Improvement: Adopting a culture of continuous improvement allows for the identification of areas where change can lead to positive outcomes without compromising stability.
04. Risk Management: Evaluating and managing risks associated with change can alleviate concerns and facilitate a more gradual and controlled transition.

In conclusion, while comfort with the status quo offers stability and familiarity, it's essential to strike a balance. Embracing change when necessary and fostering an environment that encourages innovation can lead to growth, adaptability, and long-term success.

4. Perceived Threat to Job Security:

The perceived threat to job security refers to an individual's belief or sense of insecurity regarding the continuity of their employment. This perception can arise from various factors and circumstances, leading to anxiety, stress, and concerns about the stability of one's job.

Key Aspects of Perceived Threat to Job Security:

01. Economic Factors: Economic downturns, industry fluctuations, or financial challenges within an organization can contribute to perceptions of job insecurity.
02. Organizational Restructuring: News or rumors about organizational restructuring, mergers, acquisitions, or downsizing can create uncertainties about the future of individual positions.
03. Technological Changes: The implementation of new technologies, automation, or

advancements that may replace certain job functions can lead to fears of job displacement.

04. Performance Concerns: Individuals who perceive their own performance as inadequate or who receive negative feedback may feel more vulnerable to job loss.

05. Industry Trends: Changes in industry trends, market demands, or shifts in consumer behavior can impact job security, particularly in sectors sensitive to external influences.

Effects of Perceived Threat to Job Security:

01. Stress and Anxiety: Individuals experiencing perceived job insecurity often face heightened levels of stress and anxiety, impacting overall well-being.

02. Decreased Morale and Productivity: Job insecurity can lead to decreased morale and reduced productivity as employees may become preoccupied with concerns about their future.

03. Reduced Job Satisfaction: The fear of job loss may contribute to decreased job satisfaction, affecting an individual's engagement and commitment to their role.

04. Impact on Mental Health: Prolonged perceptions of job insecurity can have negative effects on mental health, potentially leading to issues such as depression or burnout.

Mitigating Perceived Threat to Job Security:

01. Transparent Communication: Transparent communication from organizational leadership about the company's financial health, future plans, and potential changes can help alleviate uncertainties.

02. Skill Development and Training: Offering opportunities for skill development and training can empower employees to adapt to changing job requirements and enhance their job security.

03. Recognition of Contributions: Recognizing and appreciating employees for their

contributions can help boost morale and
foster a sense of value within the
organization.
04. Job Redesign and Reskilling: Organizations
can explore job redesign options and invest in
reskilling programs to align employees' skills
with evolving organizational needs.
05. Employee Assistance Programs (EAPs):
Implementing EAPs or support services can
provide employees with resources for
managing stress and anxiety related to job
security concerns.

Addressing perceived threats to job security requires
a proactive and supportive approach from both
individuals and organizations. Open communication,
skill development, and a commitment to employee
well-being are key elements in fostering a more
secure and resilient workforce.

5. Lack of Understanding:
   The lack of understanding refers to a situation
where individuals or groups lack comprehension or
awareness about a particular subject, concept, or
perspective. It can manifest in various contexts,

leading to miscommunication, confusion, and a failure to grasp the intricacies of the matter at hand.

Key Aspects of Lack of Understanding:

1. Miscommunication: Misinterpretation or incomplete communication can contribute to a lack of understanding among individuals or within an organization.

2. Unfamiliarity with Concepts: Lack of exposure or knowledge about specific concepts, technologies, or ideas can hinder a person's ability to understand or engage with them effectively.

3. Differing Perspectives: Varied experiences, backgrounds, or cultural differences can lead to differing perspectives and contribute to a lack of shared understanding among individuals or groups.

4. Incomplete Information: Limited or incomplete information about a topic can result in gaps in

understanding, hindering the ability to make informed decisions.

5. Educational Gaps: Differences in educational backgrounds, levels of expertise, or access to information can contribute to varying degrees of understanding within a group.

Effects of Lack of Understanding:

1. Confusion: Individuals experiencing a lack of understanding may feel confused, uncertain, or unable to make sense of the information presented to them.

2. Misalignment: Lack of understanding can lead to misalignment of goals, expectations, or priorities among individuals or teams, impacting overall coordination.

3. Errors and Mistakes: Misinterpretation or lack of clarity can result in errors, mistakes, or suboptimal outcomes in tasks or projects.

4. Strained Relationships: Communication breakdowns due to lack of understanding may strain relationships, both personal and professional.

5. Missed Opportunities: Failure to comprehend opportunities or possibilities may lead to missed chances for innovation, collaboration, or improvement.

Addressing Lack of Understanding:
- Clear Communication: Encouraging clear, concise, and open communication helps minimize misunderstandings and ensures that information is conveyed effectively.
- Education and Training: Providing education and training programs can enhance individuals' understanding of specific topics, tools, or methodologies.
- Active Listening: Promoting active listening skills helps individuals better comprehend information and fosters a culture of attentive and engaged communication.
- Diversity and Inclusion: Embracing diversity and inclusion promotes a range of perspectives, contributing to a more

comprehensive understanding within a group
or organization.

- Feedback Mechanisms: Establishing
  feedback mechanisms allows for continuous
  evaluation and adjustment, reducing the
  likelihood of misunderstandings.
- Encouraging Questions: Creating an
  environment where individuals feel
  comfortable asking questions fosters a culture
  of curiosity and continual learning.

Addressing the lack of understanding involves a
commitment to effective communication, education,
and fostering an environment where diverse
perspectives are valued. By actively promoting
clarity, learning, and open dialogue, individuals and
organizations can work towards enhancing overall
understanding and collaboration.

6. Past Negative Experiences:
   Past negative experiences refer to adverse or
unfavorable situations that individuals have
encountered in their personal or professional lives.
These experiences can leave a lasting impact,

influencing emotions, behavior, and perspectives in
the present and future.

Key Aspects of Past Negative Experiences:

1. Emotional Residue: Negative experiences often
leave emotional residue, such as feelings of
disappointment, fear, or trauma, which can influence
how individuals approach similar situations.

2. Cognitive Impact: Negative experiences can
shape cognitive patterns, leading to biases,
pessimism, or defensive attitudes when facing
circumstances that resemble the past negative event.

3. Impact on Trust: Trust can be eroded by past
negative experiences, making individuals more
cautious or hesitant in forming new relationships or
entering into new ventures.

4. Influence on Decision-Making: Past negative
experiences may influence decision-making
processes, with individuals being more risk-averse
or resistant to change to avoid potential recurrence
of negative outcomes.

5. Coping Mechanisms: Individuals may develop specific coping mechanisms in response to past negative experiences, which can either be adaptive or maladaptive in addressing current challenges.

Effects of Past Negative Experiences:

01. Fear of Rejection or Failure: Past failures or rejection can contribute to a fear of experiencing similar outcomes, potentially hindering individuals from taking risks or pursuing new opportunities.
02. Avoidance Behaviors: Individuals may exhibit avoidance behaviors to steer clear of situations that trigger memories of past negative experiences, limiting personal or professional growth.
03. Impact on Relationships: Past negative experiences can impact interpersonal relationships, making it challenging to trust others, express vulnerability, or engage in open communication.
04. Self-Doubt: Individuals who have faced criticism or negative feedback in the past may struggle with self-doubt, questioning their abilities and worth.

05. Residual Stress: Lingering stress from past negative experiences can contribute to ongoing mental health challenges, affecting overall well-being.

Coping Strategies for Dealing with Past Negative Experiences:

1. Reflection and Self-Awareness: Reflecting on past experiences and developing self-awareness helps individuals understand how these experiences have shaped their perceptions and behaviors.

2. Seeking Support: Seeking support from friends, family, or professionals can provide a safe space to share emotions, gain perspective, and receive guidance on coping strategies.

3. Therapeutic Interventions: Professional therapy, counseling, or other therapeutic interventions can offer targeted strategies for processing and overcoming the impact of past negative experiences.

4. Positive Reinforcement: Focusing on positive aspects, achievements, and strengths can help counteract negative self-perceptions resulting from past experiences.

5. Gradual Exposure: Gradual exposure to situations that resemble past negative experiences, in a controlled and supportive environment, can facilitate desensitization and build resilience.

6. Learning and Growth Mindset: Adopting a learning and growth mindset involves viewing past negative experiences as opportunities for personal and professional development rather than fixed indicators of one's capabilities.

While past negative experiences can be challenging, individuals have the capacity for resilience and growth. Acknowledging the impact, seeking support, and actively engaging in strategies to cope and overcome can contribute to a more positive and adaptive mindset for the future.

Addressing resistance to change involves proactive communication, engagement, and strategies to mitigate concerns. Successful change management includes:

1. Clear Communication:
   - Clearly articulate the reasons for change, the benefits, and the expected outcomes.
   - Provide regular updates to keep everyone informed about the progress of the change initiative.

2. Inclusive Decision-Making:
   - Involve employees in the decision-making process to give them a sense of ownership and control.

3. Employee Education and Training:
   - Provide training and support to help employees develop the skills needed for the changes.
   - Address misconceptions and offer opportunities for learning.

4. Leadership Support:
   - Ensure visible and consistent support from top leadership to inspire confidence in the change process.

- Leaders should actively communicate and embody the values and vision associated with the changes.

5. Acknowledgment of Concerns:
   - Acknowledge and address concerns raised by employees.
   - Encourage open dialogue and provide forums for discussion to express concerns.

6. Gradual Implementation:
   - Implement changes incrementally when feasible, allowing individuals to adapt gradually.
   - Celebrate small victories and milestones to build positive momentum.

Understanding and managing resistance to change is a critical aspect of successful organizational transformation. By addressing concerns, fostering a positive and inclusive environment, and providing the necessary support, organizations can navigate change more effectively and increase the likelihood of successful implementation.

B. <u>FINANCIAL CONSTRAINTS.</u>

Financial constraints refer to limitations or restrictions on an organization's financial resources that may impede its ability to pursue certain activities, investments, or strategies. These constraints can arise from various factors, impacting the organization's financial flexibility and influencing decision-making processes.

Common sources of financial constraints include:

1. Limited Capital: Insufficient funds or restricted access to capital can constrain an organization's ability to invest in new projects, research, development, or expansion.

2.High Levels of Debt: Excessive debt can lead to high-interest payments, reducing the available funds for other essential activities and limiting financial maneuverability.

3. Cash Flow Issues: Challenges in managing and maintaining positive cash flow can restrict the organization's ability to cover operational expenses,

invest in growth, or respond to unforeseen circumstances.

4. Market Volatility: Economic fluctuations and market uncertainties can impact revenue streams and affect the organization's financial stability.

5. Competitive Pressure: Intense competition may force organizations to allocate resources defensively, limiting their ability to make strategic investments or take calculated risks.

6. Regulatory Compliance Costs: Adhering to regulatory requirements can impose additional financial burdens on organizations, affecting their ability to allocate resources to other areas.

7. Global Economic Conditions: Economic downturns or geopolitical events on a global scale can affect consumer demand, disrupt supply chains, and create financial challenges for organizations.

8. Limited Access to Financing Options: Difficulty in securing loans, attracting investors, or accessing

alternative financing options can constrain an
organization's financial capabilities.

Addressing financial constraints often involves
strategic financial management and
decision-making. Organizations may employ various
strategies to navigate financial challenges:

1. Cost Reduction Strategies:
- Implementing cost-cutting measures to optimize
operational efficiency and reduce unnecessary
expenses.
2. Diversification of Revenue Streams:
- Exploring new markets, products, or services to
diversify revenue sources and reduce dependence on
a single income stream.

3. Efficient Capital Allocation:
- Prioritizing investments based on their potential
return on investment and aligning them with
organizational goals.

4. Debt Management:

- Proactively managing debt levels, refinancing when feasible, and negotiating favorable terms to improve financial flexibility.

5. Strategic Partnerships:
- Collaborating with strategic partners or seeking joint ventures to share costs and resources.

6. Innovation and Adaptation:
- Embracing innovation and adapting to changing market conditions to stay competitive and capture new opportunities.

By understanding and addressing financial constraints, organizations can enhance their financial resilience, improve strategic decision-making, and position themselves for sustainable long-term success.

C. <u>REGULATORY COMPLIANCE.</u>

Regulatory compliance refers to the adherence of an organization to laws, regulations, guidelines, and standards relevant to its industry and operations. Ensuring regulatory compliance is essential for businesses to operate legally, ethically, and responsibly. These regulations are imposed by government authorities, industry bodies, or other governing bodies to protect the interests of various stakeholders, maintain fair competition, and address broader societal concerns.

Key aspects of regulatory compliance include:

1. Legal Obligations:
   - Organizations must comply with laws and statutes at local, national, and international levels that govern their activities.

2. Industry Standards:
   - Compliance with industry-specific standards and guidelines is often mandatory to ensure product quality, safety, and ethical practices.

3. Environmental Regulations:
   - Compliance with environmental laws and regulations, including waste disposal, emissions, and sustainable practices.

4. Data Protection and Privacy:

- Ensuring the protection of customer and employee data in accordance with privacy laws and regulations.

5. Labor Laws:
   - Adherence to regulations governing employment practices, including wages, working hours, and occupational health and safety.

6. Financial Reporting:
   - Compliance with financial reporting standards and regulations to ensure accurate and transparent financial disclosures.

7. Anti-corruption Laws:
   - Compliance with anti-corruption and bribery laws to prevent unethical business practices.

8. Consumer Protection:
   - Adhering to laws that protect consumers, covering areas such as product safety, advertising practices, and fair business dealings.

9. Health and Safety Regulations:

- Ensuring a safe working environment and compliance with health and safety regulations to protect employees.

10. Securities and Exchange Regulations:
   - Compliance with regulations governing the issuance and trading of securities, if applicable to the organization.

Consequences of non-compliance can include legal penalties, fines, damage to reputation, and operational disruptions. Therefore, organizations typically establish compliance programs, engage in regular audits, and appoint compliance officers to monitor and ensure adherence to applicable regulations.

Key components of effective regulatory compliance management include:

1. Risk Assessment: Identifying potential compliance risks and evaluating their impact on the organization.

2. Policy Development: Developing and implementing policies and procedures to ensure compliance with relevant regulations.

3. Training and Education: Providing training to employees to ensure awareness and understanding of compliance requirements.

4. Monitoring and Auditing: Conducting regular internal audits to assess compliance levels and identify areas for improvement.

5. Documentation and Reporting: Maintaining accurate records and reporting mechanisms to demonstrate compliance efforts.

6. Continuous Improvement: Adapting to changes in regulations and continuously improving compliance processes.

Effective regulatory compliance
In conclusion, overcoming challenges in sustainable business practices requires a strategic and collaborative approach. By addressing resistance to change, finding innovative financial solutions, and navigating regulatory compliance with foresight,

organizations can pave the way for long-term success in their sustainability endeavors. These challenges, when approached as opportunities for growth and improvement, can lead to a more resilient, responsible, and sustainable business model.

CHAPTER EIGHT.

CASE STUDIES- LEARNING FROM SUCCESS AND FAILURE IN SUSTAINABLE BUSINESS PRACTICES.

Success and failure in sustainable business practices can be defined by the impact an organization has on environmental, social, and economic aspects, as well as its ability to align sustainability with long-term business goals. Here's an overview:

SUCCESS IN SUSTAINABLE BUSINESS PRACTICES.

1. Positive Environmental Impact:

   - Successful companies reduce their environmental footprint through initiatives such as carbon reduction, energy efficiency, waste reduction, and sustainable sourcing.

2. Social Responsibility:
   - Companies demonstrate social responsibility by fostering fair labor practices, promoting diversity and inclusion, ensuring safe working conditions, and contributing to community development.

3. Economic Resilience:
   - Integrating sustainability into business strategies can lead to economic resilience through cost savings, efficiency gains, and the ability to adapt to changing market expectations.

4. Innovation and Adaptability:
   - Successful organizations leverage sustainability for innovation, introducing eco-friendly products, implementing green technologies, and adapting to emerging sustainability trends.

5. Positive Brand Image and Reputation:
   - Companies that excel in sustainable practices build a positive brand image and reputation. This can attract environmentally conscious consumers, investors, and top talent.

6. Compliance with Standards and Regulations:

- Adhering to environmental, social, and economic standards and regulations demonstrates a commitment to ethical business practices and legal compliance.

FAILURE IN SUSTAINABLE BUSINESS PRACTICES.

1. Environmental Harm:
   - Failure may involve actions that cause environmental harm, such as pollution, deforestation, or irresponsible resource extraction.

2. Ethical Lapses and Unethical Practices:
   - Engaging in unethical practices, such as greenwashing or misleading claims about sustainability efforts, can lead to reputational damage and legal consequences.

3. Social Issues and Labor Violations:
   - Companies may fail in sustainable practices if they neglect social issues, engage in unfair labor practices, or contribute to human rights violations within their supply chains.

4. Resistance to Change:

- Failure to address resistance to sustainability initiatives within the organization can impede progress and lead to the abandonment of sustainable practices.

5. Financial Instability:
   - A lack of financial viability in implementing sustainable practices or failure to see the economic benefits can lead to financial instability.

6. Lack of Transparency:
   - Companies that fail to communicate transparently about their sustainability efforts, progress, and setbacks may face trust issues with stakeholders.

7. Non-Compliance and Legal Consequences:
   - Failure to comply with environmental, social, and economic regulations can result in legal consequences, fines, and reputational damage.

8. Ignoring Stakeholder Expectations:
   - Neglecting the expectations of key stakeholders, including customers, employees, and investors, can

lead to dissatisfaction and a negative impact on the company's bottom line.

Key Considerations:

1. Integrated Approach: Success involves integrating sustainability into the core of the business rather than treating it as a separate initiative.

2. Long-Term Vision: Successful organizations have a long-term vision that aligns sustainability with overall business objectives.

3. Adaptability and Continuous Improvement: Continuous improvement, learning from setbacks, and adapting to changing circumstances are essential for sustainable success.

Ultimately, success in sustainable business practices goes beyond meeting minimum standards; it involves creating positive, lasting impacts on the environment, society, and the organization's overall performance. Failure, on the other hand, often stems from a lack of commitment, transparency, or ethical considerations.

A. <u>SUCCESSFUL COMPANIES: EMBRACING SUSTAINABLE PRACTICES</u>.

Successful companies embracing sustainable practices demonstrate a commitment to environmental, social, and economic responsibility while also achieving business success. These companies serve as examples of how integrating sustainability into their core strategies can lead to positive outcomes. Here are a few noteworthy examples:

1. Patagonia:

   -Key Features: Patagonia, a renowned outdoor apparel company, is a pioneer in sustainable business practices. It focuses on product durability, ethical sourcing, and fair labor practices. The "Worn Wear" program encourages customers to buy used clothing, promoting longevity and reducing environmental impact.

   -Impact: Patagonia's commitment to sustainability has built a loyal customer base, enhanced its brand image, and showcased that environmentally responsible practices can align with profitability.

2. Unilever:
   - Key Features: Unilever has integrated
sustainability into its business strategy through the
"Sustainable Living Plan." This ambitious plan
includes goals like sourcing 100% sustainable palm
oil and achieving zero net emissions by 2039.
Unilever emphasizes responsible consumption and
production, social impact, and environmental
stewardship.
   - Impact: Unilever's sustainability efforts have
contributed to brand value, cost savings, and a
positive image. The company showcases how
sustainability can drive innovation and business
success.

3. Tesla:
   - Key Features: Tesla, led by Elon Musk, has
revolutionized the automotive industry with a focus
on electric vehicles and renewable energy solutions.
Tesla's commitment to sustainability extends beyond
products to include the development of energy
storage solutions and solar technologies.
   - Impact: Tesla's success not only disrupted
traditional automotive markets but also set new
standards for environmental responsibility in the

industry. The company has demonstrated that sustainable practices can lead to market leadership and innovation.

4. Interface, Inc.:
   - Key Features: Interface, a global modular flooring company, has been a leader in sustainable business practices. The company has set ambitious goals, including achieving "Mission Zero" – a commitment to eliminate any negative environmental impact by 2020. Interface emphasizes sustainable materials, energy efficiency, and closed-loop manufacturing processes.
   - Impact: Interface's sustainability efforts have not only reduced its environmental impact but also improved operational efficiency and positioned the company as an industry leader in sustainability.

5. Danone:
   - Key Features: Danone, a multinational food-products corporation, emphasizes social and environmental responsibility. The company has a dual commitment to business success and social progress, focusing on issues like water scarcity, carbon reduction, and promoting healthier food options.

-Impact: Danone's sustainable practices have contributed to its positive brand image, attracting consumers who align with its values. The company demonstrates how a commitment to sustainability can be integrated into the core of its business model.

These companies showcase that successful business outcomes and sustainability are not mutually exclusive. By aligning sustainability with their overall business strategies, they not only reduce their environmental footprint but also enhance brand reputation, attract consumers, and drive innovation. These examples inspire other organizations to consider sustainable practices as integral to their long-term success.

B. LESSONS LEARNED FROM FAILURES COMPANIES.

1. Volkswagen's Emissions Scandal: Ignoring Environmental Standards

- Volkswagen faced a major setback when it was revealed that the company had manipulated emissions tests on their diesel vehicles. This scandal not only led to substantial financial losses and legal consequences but also severely damaged the company's reputation. The lesson here is clear: unethical practices, especially related to environmental standards, can have severe consequences.

2. BP Deepwater Horizon Oil Spill: Environmental and Reputational Catastrophe
   - The Deepwater Horizon oil spill in the Gulf of Mexico had devastating consequences for BP. The environmental damage, loss of lives, and economic impact highlighted the critical importance of stringent safety measures and the need for responsible environmental stewardship in the oil and gas industry.

3. Wells Fargo's Account Scandal: Ethical Lapses in Banking.
   - Wells Fargo faced a major scandal when it was revealed that employees had created unauthorized accounts to meet sales targets. This highlighted the importance of ethical business practices, as the bank faced legal repercussions, financial penalties, and a damaged reputation.

Key Takeaways:

1. Integrating Sustainability:
  - Successful companies integrate sustainability into their core business strategies, demonstrating that environmental and social responsibility can align with profitability.

2. Transparency and Ethical Practices:
  - Failures often result from a lack of transparency, ethical lapses, or non-compliance with regulations. Ethical conduct is crucial for long-term success.

3. Customer and Stakeholder Trust:
  - Building and maintaining trust with customers and stakeholders is essential. Successful companies prioritize open communication and ethical behavior.

4. Adaptability and Innovation:
  - Sustainability success stories often involve companies that embrace adaptability and innovation. They are willing to challenge conventional practices and explore new, sustainable solutions.

In conclusion, examining case studies of both successful and failed attempts at sustainable business practices provides valuable insights for organizations striving for long-term success. These examples illustrate that sustainability is not only a moral imperative but also a strategic business imperative with the potential to drive innovation, resilience, and lasting positive impact.

CHAPTER NINE.

IMPLEMENTING SUSTAINABLE PRACTICES IN SMALL BUSINESS.

In this chapter, we explore the practical aspects of integrating sustainable practices into small businesses. Recognizing the unique challenges and opportunities that small businesses face, we focus on scalable strategies and available resources for owners aiming to foster sustainability and achieve long-term success.

A. SCALABLE STRATEGIES.

1. Energy Efficiency:
   - Scalable Approach: Implementing energy-efficient practices, such as using LED lighting, optimizing heating and cooling systems, and adopting energy-efficient appliances, can lead to cost savings and reduced environmental impact.

2. Waste Reduction and Recycling:
   - Scalable Approach: Introduce waste reduction initiatives by promoting recycling, minimizing single-use items, and establishing partnerships with local recycling services. This not only benefits the environment but can also enhance the business's reputation.

 3. Local and Sustainable Sourcing:
   - Scalable Approach: Embrace local and sustainable sourcing practices by establishing partnerships with local suppliers and incorporating eco-friendly products into the inventory. Communicating this commitment to customers can attract environmentally conscious consumers.

4. Employee Engagement:
   - Scalable Approach: Engage employees in sustainability initiatives by fostering a culture of environmental responsibility. Implement training programs, encourage energy-saving habits, and involve employees in decision-making regarding sustainable practices.

5. Community Involvement:

- Scalable Approach: Participate in community initiatives or support local environmental projects. This not only contributes to community development but also enhances the company's reputation as a socially responsible business.

B. <u>RESOURCES FOR SMALL BUSINESS OWNERS.</u>

1. Government Grants and Incentives:

- Available Resources: Explore government programs that offer grants, tax incentives, or subsidies for businesses implementing sustainable practices. Many governments provide financial support to encourage environmentally friendly initiatives.

2. Sustainable Business Networks:

- Available Resources: Join sustainable business networks and associations. These groups often provide resources, guidance, and networking opportunities for small businesses looking to integrate sustainability into their operations.

3. Online Sustainability Tools:
   - Available Resources: Utilize online tools and platforms that offer sustainability assessments, carbon footprint calculators, and guidance on sustainable practices. These tools can help small businesses measure their impact and identify areas for improvement.

4. Local Sustainability Programs:
   - Available Resources: Explore local sustainability programs or initiatives offered by municipalities, chambers of commerce, or non-profit organizations. These programs may provide support, recognition, and resources for businesses committed to sustainability.

5. Collaboration with Suppliers:
   - *Available Resources:* Collaborate with suppliers who share a commitment to sustainability. Some suppliers may offer resources, guidance, or incentives to encourage sustainable practices in their supply chain.

6. Sustainability Certifications:
   - Available Resources: Consider obtaining sustainability certifications relevant to the industry.

Certifications, such as B Corp certification or eco-labels, can enhance the business's credibility and attract environmentally conscious customers.

In conclusion, implementing sustainable practices in small businesses requires a strategic and scalable approach. By focusing on energy efficiency, waste reduction, local sourcing, employee engagement, and community involvement, small businesses can make meaningful contributions to sustainability. Leveraging available resources, including government incentives, sustainable networks, online tools, local programs, supplier collaborations, and certifications, empowers small business owners to navigate the path towards a more sustainable and successful future.

CHAPTER TEN.

CONCLUSION.

EMBRACING SUSTAINABLE BUSINESS PRACTICES FOR LONG-TERM SUCCESS.

As we conclude our exploration of sustainable business practices and their role in achieving long-term success, it's crucial to recap the key points and offer encouragement for the transformative journey that lies ahead.

A. RECAP OF KEY POINTS.
1. Integrated Approach:
   - Successful sustainable practices go beyond compliance; they are integrated into the core of the business, shaping its culture, operations, and strategic decisions.

2. Environmental Stewardship:
   - Companies that prioritize environmental sustainability contribute to a healthier planet, reduce

their ecological footprint, and position themselves as responsible global citizens.

3. Social Responsibility:
   - Socially responsible practices, including fair labor practices, diversity and inclusion, and community engagement, foster positive relationships with stakeholders and build trust.

4. Economic Resilience:
   - Integrating sustainability into business strategies can lead to economic resilience, cost savings, and increased competitiveness in a rapidly evolving market.

5. Innovation and Adaptability:
   - Sustainable companies embrace innovation and adaptability, challenging conventional practices and exploring new, environmentally friendly solutions.

6. Transparency and Trust:
   - Transparency builds trust. Communicating openly about sustainability efforts, progress, and setbacks enhances credibility and strengthens relationships with stakeholders.

B. <u>ENCOURAGEMENT FOR SUSTAINABLE BUSINESS PRACTICES TRANSFORMATION</u>.

As you embark on or continue your sustainable business journey, consider the following words of encouragement:

1. Start Small, Think Big:
  - Begin by implementing manageable sustainable practices that align with your business's values and goals. Gradual steps can lead to transformative change over time.

2. Engage Stakeholders:
  - Foster a sense of shared responsibility by involving employees, customers, suppliers, and local communities in your sustainability initiatives. Collaboration enhances collective impact.

3. Learn from Setbacks:
  - Sustainable transformation may encounter challenges. View setbacks as opportunities to learn, adapt, and refine your approach. Resilience is key to long-term success.

4. Celebrate Achievements:
   - Recognize and celebrate milestones, whether big or small. Acknowledging achievements boosts morale, reinforces commitment, and inspires continuous improvement.

5. Stay Informed and Adaptive:
   - Keep abreast of evolving sustainability trends, regulations, and best practices. An adaptive approach ensures your business remains at the forefront of sustainable innovation.

6. Inspire Others:
   - Share your sustainability journey with others in your industry and community. Inspiring fellow businesses to adopt sustainable practices creates a positive ripple effect.

7. Measure and Communicate Impact:
   - Use metrics to measure the impact of your sustainability initiatives. Clear communication about your achievements enhances accountability and builds trust with stakeholders.

8. Embrace a Circular Economy:

   - Consider adopting circular economy practices where resources are used efficiently, waste is minimized, and products are designed for longevity. This holistic approach contributes to a regenerative and sustainable business model.

In closing, the pursuit of sustainable business practices is not only a commitment to the well-being of our planet and society but also a strategic investment in the longevity and success of your business. As you navigate the path toward sustainability, remember that every eco-conscious decision contributes to a more sustainable, resilient, and prosperous future. May your sustainable journey be both fulfilling and transformative.